KT-554-108

Business-focused IT

and service excellence

David Miller

 BCS

NORWICH CITY COLLEGE

Stock No.	234 406	
Class	658.4038 MIL	
Cat.	3UL	Proc	A2

Copyright © 2008 David Miller

The rights of David Miller to be identified as the author of this work have been asserted in accordance with the Copyright, Design, and Patents Act 1998.

First Published in Great Britain in 2005 by ITDYNAMICS™ Ltd

ITDYNAMICS™ is a registered trademark.

All rights reserved. Apart from any fair dealing for the purposes of research or private study, or criticism or review, as permitted by the Copyright Designs and Patents Act 1988, no part of this publication may be reproduced, stored or transmitted in any form or by any means, except with the prior permission in writing of the Publisher, or in the case of reprographic reproduction, in accordance with the terms of the licences issued by the Copyright Licensing Agency. Enquiries for permission to reproduce material outside those terms should be directed to the Publisher.

BCS
Publishing and Information Products
First Floor, Block D
North Star House
North Star Avenue
Swindon
SN2 1FA
UK

www.bcs.org

ISBN 978-1-902505-88-6

British Cataloguing in Publication Data.
A CIP catalogue record for this book is available at the British Library.

All trademarks, registered names etc. acknowledged in this publication are to be the property of their respective owners.

Disclaimer:
The views expressed in this book are of the author(s) and do not necessarily reflect the views of BCS except where explicitly stated as such.
Although every care has been taken by the authors and BCS in the preparation of the publication, no warranty is given by the authors or BCS as Publisher as to the accuracy or completeness of the information contained within it and neither the authors nor BCS shall be responsible or liable for any loss or damage whatsoever arising by virtue of such information or any instructions or advice contained within this publication or by any of the aforementioned.

Typeset by Lapiz Digital Services.
Printed and bound in Great Britain by Antony Rowe Ltd, Chippenham, Wiltshire.

Business-focused IT

and service excellence

234 406

The British Computer Society

BCS is the leading professional body for the IT industry. With members in over 100 countries, the BCS is the professional and learned Society in the field of computers and information systems.

The BCS is responsible for setting standards for the IT profession. It is also leading the change in public perception and appreciation of the economic and social importance of professionally managed IT projects and programmes. In this capacity, the Society advises, informs and persuades industry and government on successful IT implementation.

IT is affecting every part of our lives and that is why the BCS is determined to promote IT as the profession of the 21st century.

Joining BCS

BCS qualifications, products and services are designed with your career plans in mind. We not only provide essential recognition through professional qualifications but also offer many other useful benefits to our members at every level.

BCS Membership demonstrates your commitment to professional development. It helps to set you apart from other IT practitioners and provides industry recognition of your skills and experience. Employers and customers increasingly require proof of professional qualifications and competence. Professional membership confirms your competence and integrity and sets an independent standard that people can trust. Professional Membership (MBCS) is the pathway to Chartered IT Professional (CITP) Status.

www.bcs.org/membership

Further Information

Further information about BCS can be obtained from: BCS, First Floor, Block D, North Star House, North Star Avenue, Swindon, SN2 1FA, UK.

Telephone: 0845 300 4417 (UK only) or + 44 (0)1793 417 424 (overseas)

Contact: www.bcs.org/contact

Contents

Contents

List of Figures

Author

David Miller is a consultant and interim manager and an authority on service excellence. He operates at board and senior management levels planning and leading large-scale change across business and IT. Assignments typically involve managing complex stakeholder relationships and achieving business improvement by introducing the latest business practices, structural and process change and service improvement. He has worked with a number of major companies in the public, private and 'not for profit' sectors frequently taking national and global line management and change management responsibilities. He has worked in the USA, Europe and the Middle East.

He was an IT Manager for many years and has held director-level positions at the Computer Sciences Corporation and British Rail, and he is now the Managing Director at ITDYNAMICS™. David Miller is a Chartered Engineer, a Chartered IT Professional, a Chartered Marketer, a Fellow of the British Computer Society, a Fellow of the Institution of Engineering and Technology, a Fellow of the Institute of Business Consultancy, a Fellow of the Chartered Institute of Marketing, a Fellow of the Royal Society for the encouragement of Arts, Manufactures and Commerce (RSA), a Member of the Institute of Directors and a Liveryman of the Worshipful Company of Management Consultants.

Acknowledgements

I wish to acknowledge the people that have influenced and helped me to develop my views on 'Business-focused IT'. These people include all of the employers and clients over the years that have helped me to understand the needs of business, work colleagues and associates from whom I have been able to learn, authors whose books I have read and valued, as well as the vendors of methodologies who insist that success must be judged by assessing compliance with their process rather than on outcomes. Finally, I acknowledge the body of knowledge and standards of professionalism of the organisations and their members that have bestowed fellowship upon me.

David Miller

Abbreviations

CEO	Chief executive officer
CFO	Chief financial officer
CIO	Chief information officer
CMDB	Configuration management database
CMS	Configuration management system
COBIT	Control Objectives for Information and Related Technologies
EFQM	European Foundation for Quality Management
IPR	Intellectual property rights
ITIL	Information Technology Infrastructure Library
KPI	Key performance indicator
NPD	New product development
PIR	Post implementation review
PFEST	Political, fiscal, environmental, sociological and technological influences
ROI	Return on investment
SLA	Service-level agreement
SQM	Service quality model
UHC	Ultimate holding company
UML	Unified Modeling Language

Preface

This is the sequel to the book *Business-focused IT – How brand value enhances IT product and service excellence* which was published by ITDYNAMICS™ in 2005 and which was based upon the author's experiences of working with businesses to help them to deliver major change programmes, realign their IT, help them to define and deliver IT performance improvement programmes and help them to achieve product and service excellence. Both the businesses and their IT services organisations felt they had achieved levels of satisfaction amongst their stakeholders that were not previously thought possible. In redefining service excellence we heightened the awareness amongst our clients of a 'perception gap' between what service providers think they are delivering and what the businesses think they are experiencing: this awareness enabled them to succeed in areas where they had previously failed. The book was well received in public and single-company seminars and at conferences. We also understand that it has become something of a 'cult read'. Since publication, a number of organisations including the BCS, The IET, the Institute of Directors and various government departments in the UK have called for more business focus in IT. Since the first edition of *Business-focused IT* was published, the latest version of the Skills Framework for the Information Age (SFIAplus3) has been released which incorporates a broader range of skills than was ever previously considered necessary and so now extending beyond the core IT skills. Also since the first edition, the third version of the Information Technology Infrastructure Library (ITIL v3) has been launched and borrows language from the first edition of *Business-focused IT*. It acknowledges a need for business focus, recognises that customers do not buy products but try to satisfy their needs, expresses the importance of outcomes rather than just process and recognises that there is a blurring of the divide between IT and the business. Although ITIL v3 is still focused on IT operations it is a restructuring of the IT service management framework which now more neatly aligns with the ITDYNAMICS™ assessment framework. This second edition, *Business-focused IT and service excellence,* now moves the thinking on still further showing not only how far we still have to travel but how much more can be achieved. Much good work has been done by groups and standards bodies to create 'how to' methodologies and to establish ways in which practitioners can gain recognition for their skills in using them. As these works are no longer insignificant in terms of their size, because changes in technology lead to changes in standards and methods and because measuring compliance with these standards or methods does not guarantee that business needs and concerns are being met, it is the author's contention that business and IT also need a quick way to assess the effectiveness of what is being delivered that is independent of the methods used. The business-focused IT frameworks included in this second edition provide for this.

The first book was written as business collateral and placed a marker in the ground for IT service excellence. It briefly dealt with the assessment framework for the service engine and the essentials of the assessment process. We have seen the impact this had on the industry. This second edition is more comprehensive: it incorporates new business-focused tools including the ITDYNAMICS™ service excellence model, an expanded version of the assessment framework for the service engine, the ITDYNAMICS™ governance framework, a new maturity model and more. We have written the book such that the principles can be applied by any service provider (i.e. not just IT services providers) and so that anyone in a business can derive some benefit from the ideas. It contains sufficient information for both service providers and businesses to assess the effectiveness of their information services, identify major shortcomings, and design and implement compelling performance improvement programmes. In short, whether you want to know how well your services are being received, or how well your service provider is performing, we hope this book will provide some answers. The focus then for this second edition is the IT professional who wishes to improve the delivery of some or all IT services, the business manager who aspires to receiving an IT service that better meets the needs of the business regardless of who is providing it and to those who simply wish to understand the impact of this business-focused approach. For some this will disappoint because it calls for a different literacy style, more broadsheet than tabloid, but the increased content allows you to form your own opinions and adapt the approach to meet your own specific needs.

As with the first edition, the book does not claim to provide detailed instructions of how to do anything; it is not a 'how to do it' technical manual. It does not replace any methodologies or other frameworks such as PRINCE2 or ITIL but it does position some of these within the context of the business. Neither is the book written with any particular technologies in mind; we hope that the principles behind this book and the messages it contains will therefore be relevant for some time.

The book is a plea to look at service through the eyes of the business customer and so to reconsider what skills are important to service providers. Based upon observing consistently high-performing organisations in client assignments delivering innovative and highly acclaimed IT strategies, major change programmes and service improvement, this second edition is a more detailed explanation of an approach which has gained credibility in only a few months. It is based now as before on real assignments, on extensive experience of the principal methods and methodologies, substantial research, our current business and legal environment, likely technological and business trends and professional and business feedback. This is not a methodology; in fact part of the inspiration for this was the rejection of every over-engineered and prescriptive methodology ever devised.

1 Service

Most of us in IT have always been fortunate enough to work for IT organisations that have made every effort to deliver high levels of service, whether this was helping to shape business and IT strategy, defining detailed requirements, developing or delivering solutions, managing business change, delivering services or providing support services. Over the years there have been an increasing number of methods, tools and frameworks based on industry best practice to help us. We have often measured our performance using key performance indicators (KPIs), customer satisfaction questionnaires and benchmark comparisons with other similar organisations. Some of us may even work for organisations with trophies and other awards proudly displayed in glass cabinets in the office foyer. Unfortunately none of this necessarily means that we are achieving either service excellence or high levels of business satisfaction. If you do not believe this, just ask business managers what they think about IT and you will begin to understand the nature of the mountain that IT still has to climb. If you are a business manager then you will already understand the problem and you will be aware of the importance of the need to address this in order to move the business forward. Perhaps this is why you are reading this book. Regardless of the motivation for you, the reader, we hope that you will find much amongst these pages to increase the effectiveness of IT in your business or for your customer.

THE BUSINESS MIND

In most of our buying experiences there is the expectation of how we will benefit from our investment and in most cases this is based upon assumptions that we shall be receiving something other than the core product. We have probably built up an expectation based upon what we have seen in the media and what we have heard from colleagues or friends. The marketers of the product or service will have considered the offering and how this will be structured and designed. Maybe this was a sophisticated process based upon desk-based market research, focus group analysis and trial marketing. In the case of the sometimes rather more abstract products and services, there will be a need for a salesperson to explain the benefits to the potential customer to perhaps articulate the expectation and even to build the business case for the investment.

Theodore Levitt famously suggested that customers do not buy a quarter inch drill bit for its own sake but for the quarter inch holes it makes (Levitt 1986). If this is true, customers might work out the return from investing in drill bits of varying quality (the actual size of the hole, the number of holes they are likely to be able to drill in the material they are using before they need to replace the bit, the time it will take to drill each hole etc.) or they might research other ways of making quarter inch holes with greater efficiency. If the customer is not thinking so rationally they will almost always buy the cheapest drill bits and accept the consequences. Poor investment decisions frequently lead to poor product or service. Businesses do not buy IT services for their own sake but for what they do for the business and for this reason we are seeing an upsurge in the importance of service excellence. As the lead time from initial idea, through planning, to implementation can be many months and the sales cycle from key vendors can take more than a year in some cases, it will inevitably take a long time to recover from a poor investment decision. Rarely in business as in our personal lives is there any formal post implementation review (PIR) of investments and so this change is not coming about as a result of any formal process but through less tangible means associated with need. Where there is a formal PIR it will be conducted by IT as part of some methodology and it does represent best practice to consider all aspects of a project and to feed back any possible ways in which we might improve the process for the future. The reason that businesses rarely engage in this is that their key people are usually already focusing on the next challenge. If customers are satisfied with a product or service they will tell others; if they are not satisfied they will do the same. It follows therefore that it is worth taking the effort to ensure that our business customers and users are satisfied with the business experience from the first engagement with us, through implementation, to their experiences as a user of our services. In turn this means, rather like the marketers, we must understand the business need and we must think hard about how we design the products and services that we provide so that we meet or exceed expectation by intent rather than by accident.

Whatever methods and technologies we deploy, the ultimate test is not necessarily whether the financial return is as we expected it to be or how well we adhere to best practice, but how highly the results are regarded by our stakeholders. Whilst financial and process controls may be helpful, in the real world the way in which we are mostly measured is by outcome. Some may choose to interpret this as a criticism of methodology and process; what the author says is that the success of any process can only be judged on outcome. If the outcome is unsatisfactory then we have to modify the process. This is the basis of the work of Deming at the macro level and Six Sigma at the micro level. These are measurement and feedback tools often applied in business. When we apply business focus to IT we could and often do apply these techniques but we can probably do more. We need both a macro and a micro toolset to enable us to understand how well our service is performing in terms of the extent to which it is meeting the business needs and how we might improve it.

As Levitt might have said, 'Are we getting the holes we need or just using a drill bit?'.

If the service provider gets everything right you can be sure that the business will be enjoying high levels of satisfaction; as soon as a weakness appears in any aspect of the product or service then we know that there will always be low perceptions of satisfaction amongst business stakeholders. When we understand how opinions can shift very quickly we need to have ways of monitoring every aspect of the service, from the core elements to those things that we will collectively refer to as influencing brand equity.

Kotler et al. (2002) talk about 'brand equity' as being the product of value, image and loyalty. It is ironic that in IT we deal with business and technical detail requiring intellect and precision and yet our products and services are sometimes less tangible than those that our business customers sell. IT products and services can have a complex benefit structure and if we fail to convince the business of either the potential or the efficacy of our solutions, then both the service provider and the business itself may suffer. No one doubts that we need to create brand equity in the IT sector, but knowing how to achieve this is not always well understood. We break down the many possible aspects of disenchantment that can arise between service providers and their business customers and we identify the many skills needed by IT product and services organisations to improve the situation.

You will see that it is the author's contention that most IT product and services organisations, whether selling their services commercially or providing an internal service, are almost totally IT-focused rather than business-focused. Today, IT has many methods and standards at its disposal but they are IT-focused and IT-focused organisations are only concerned with the core product or service. To be business-focused, IT organisations must respond to the same market challenges as their business counterparts, change their behaviour, use new approaches and develop new skills. This will create brand equity.

LEARNING FROM THE PAST

IT has been a disruptive force for almost 50 years. Business has been able to remove layers of management, process and cost. Business has also had to adapt to the competitive pressures such that doing nothing was never an option. The IT phenomenon has no comparison; technological change just presses on relentlessly and those organisations that do not wish to exploit these changes will cease to be competitive. Frequently, the industry becomes over-optimistic in terms of what it can deliver and we experience the consequences: the so-called initial 'dot.com boom' was a prime example of this although if we look at what is happening now, we are radically changing organisations in both the business-to-business and the business-to-consumer markets.

The IT hardware and software organisations themselves are not immune from technological change as we have seen over recent years. The best example is probably the transition of IBM to become almost exclusively an IT services provider rather than a hardware manufacturer but there are many examples of organisations being caught out by shifts in technology. During periods of rapid development in a particular market we also see rationalisation as organisations merge to create stronger businesses that are more capable of competing.

So if the IT industry becomes over-optimistic about what can be achieved, can we assume that business is the reluctant partner? The answer in the author's experience is no. Often business also has over-ambitious expectations, in fact expectation is often well in advance of what can be delivered. The number of technological solutions that have been selected that are immature and under-developed would never have been selected if it were not for over-zealous and over-confident business sponsors who had perhaps been sold an inappropriate and over-optimistic solution. The term 'vapourware' was coined to address this very phenomenon and the industry has to recognise that much damage has been done to reputations as a consequence.

IT is not the only sector to suffer from over-selling but the rapid rate of change and the intangible nature of IT solutions makes this sector particularly vulnerable. Whilst acknowledging what has been achieved by the IT sector, we must nevertheless look to do better.

The industry structure that gave rise to this situation is complex and continues to evolve. There are the vendors within the computer software and services sector. The first tier ranges from the principal hardware manufacturers, former hardware manufacturers, operating system vendors, software solutions companies and major systems integrators, service providers and telecommunications companies. Also in this group are the outsourced service providers who typically take over the IT staff and IT assets and manage them at lower cost on behalf of their business customers but who also offer a full range of products and services by developing strategic relationships with other organisations. There has been a rapid growth in offshore services providers based in countries where the cost of labour is low. These often provide the low-end horsepower for coding or call centres but the lower costs can often be offset by a higher than normal onshore management overhead. In the long run this offshore phenomenon will change as the third-world labour costs rise; they will either become less successful as the cost advantage diminishes or they will move into higher value activities but their ability to make this transition will depend upon many other factors. There is a middle tier of specialist software houses, hardware vendors and service providers. The final group consists of the many independent business and management consultants, interim managers and contractors. These people provide major industry flexibility as well as much of the intellectual horsepower when it comes to major change programmes by either providing specialist skills to other organisations or by leading business change on behalf of others.

The larger organisations, whether businesses or IT service providers, have tended towards methods, standards and 'collective best practice' of some kind. They have tended to gravitate towards methods in order to create competitive advantage, improve workforce mobility, build up a body of knowledge more quickly or to establish a minimum standard. Likewise, the UK Government has been influential in developing method, owning the brand and copyright, mandating that the methods be used on all government contracts and benefiting from the sales of training material.

Also part of the industry are the international standards bodies, government buying departments (but see the previous paragraph), professional bodies and trade associations. This group is probably more highly developed in the UK than in any other country and it will hopefully help to drive forward the business-focused changes required in this sector.

There have been two aspects of IT that stand out for the author over the last 30 years. The first is the rate of change of technology as it presses relentlessly onward (Moore's law). This has moved us from the early IT era of bespoke applications, data preparation and teams of computer operators, to the global networked and web-based solutions we see today. The second is the emergence of methodologies and standards. The earliest methods to emerge in the 1970s were in the area of business analysis. These developed into full-blown strategy and planning methodologies that integrated many of the business analysis tools developed earlier. These became prevalent in the 1980s as every major consultancy developed and branded its own methodology and used it as a differentiator for competitive advantage. Next on the scene were the systems development methodologies closely followed by the project management and programme management methods including PRINCE and MSP. Finally service management was given a methodology makeover as ITIL emerged. As methods stabilised, so national or international standards evolved. All of this has contributed to the IT and business communities gaining a greater insight into managing technology driven change. Over the years there have been a number of major surveys that have tried to establish just how successful we are at managing such projects: IT Cortex (failure rate of 80%), OASIG Study 1995 (failure rate of 70%), Chaos (Standish) Report 1995 (failure rate of 84%), KPMG Canada 1997 (failure rate of 61%), Conference Board Survey 2001 (failure rate of 40%), Robbins–Gioia 2001 (failure rate of 51%), Gartner 2005 (failure rates of 60–85%), IOD survey 2005 (failure rate of 75%). We have to be careful how we define project failure and the definitions across these various surveys did differ but it is clear that in up to 80% of cases over more than 20 years projects have consistently failed to deliver on time, cost or quality (or on all three) objectives. These surveys spanned the early stages of data processing as well as the more recent networked desktop and packaged software solutions integrated with legacy and industry-specific solutions. In many of the surveys it was noted that larger projects experienced a higher failure rate. If the author was to add his own contribution to this by considering the projects that he has been aware of over more recent years (not just projects he has managed but also those known to him that have been managed by colleagues or others and from information in the public domain) the chart would look like Figure 1.1. We can see that there would appear to be no correlation between compliance with process and project success. The author has no doubt that a sample that demonstrated that there might be some correlation could be found but that is not what this sample shows. Furthermore, many of these projects were in organisations where certain methods and standards were mandated and so the process was extensive and compliance was required.

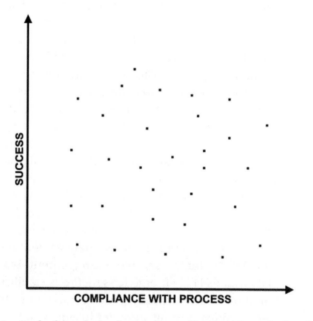

FIGURE 1.1   *Lack of correlation between compliance with method and project success*

PREPARING FOR THE FUTURE

By looking back we can understand where we have come from, how quickly we have progressed and what we have learnt along the way in terms of managing change. As we have seen, although we read a lot about how to manage change there is no evidence that we use this to guarantee project success or service excellence. Whilst some might say that technology is enabling us to automate more and what we do becomes ever more complex, others might say that the newer technologies enable us to undertake tasks more easily than ever before, for example managing, sharing and retrieving information, automating major business processes from retail to supply chain, displaying business dashboards showing real time events or business transactions etc.

As we look to the future we are seeing the rapid convergence of the information processing, telecommunications and entertainment technologies. We are seeing pervasive technology: computer systems being deployed in everyday situations such as providing directions to our destinations, controlling vehicles, controlling appliances in the home, providing the source of home entertainment etc. It is, and has always been, difficult to anticipate how progress will affect our lives and our businesses but it will happen, it will be profound and it is happening at great speed.

The rate of change is accelerating and we need a more reliable way of increasing our chances of project success when we deploy technology and deliver technology-driven business change. We know that 'business-focused IT' improves the business experience so we took the same sample of projects shown in Figure 1.1 but this time considered 'closeness to business' as opposed to 'compliance with process' and a more significant pattern emerges as shown in Figure 1.2.

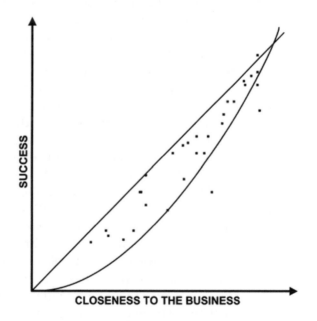

FIGURE 1.2 *Correlation between closeness to the business and project success*

Irrespective of the size of the project, we found that there is a strong correlation between these two variables. Without more research we cannot say whether the relationship is linear or some kind of exponential relationship or power law. We recognise that there is a degree of subjectivity in some of the data and in the analysis, and recognise that we must define relatively intangible terms such as 'project success' and also 'closeness to the business' but discovering this relationship is really quite exciting and one which most experienced people would say is intuitively correct. 'Business-focused IT' provides an insight into how IT services organisations can become more business-focused rather than technology-focused and hence 'closer to the business'. We explain the many ways in which this might be achieved and the ideas that can be developed and exploited in the future as businesses become more aware of how this can improve project success and service delivery. We do not feel a need to refine the power law that we can observe here but simply to gather evidence of what works and to provide ways in which a business focus can be introduced into everything that IT does.

The reasons for deploying technology in the future will, as in the past, be directed at the greatest need. As the populations of the world migrate and the world becomes less stable, we will inevitably see more of the public budget spent on intelligence, weapons, defence, immigration controls, citizen identification, custodial services, civil defence, civilian surveillance and other control systems. In countries where the population rises uncontrollably, housing and all public services will come under pressure. Technology will be used to change the way we are educated, our healthcare and what we do. Technology will be used to both develop new methods of transport and for traffic management. As oil becomes more expensive (either as a result of global conflict or through the depletion of reserves) technology will be focused on reducing fuel usage or fuel conservation, the creation of alternative fuels or technologies that reduce the need to travel. Global warming will encourage the development of technologies to manage or counter the perceived causes of climate change. There will be more breakthrough developments in healthcare and the biotechnologies to help to deal with the disease implications of the rising world population. There will be opportunities to improve the democratic processes and government itself by involving citizens in decisions and the formulation of policy. All of these global issues will drive breakthrough technologies that will have spin-off opportunities for business. In business we assume that we will be collaborating more with suppliers and others, automating more business tasks, implementing them faster and getting it right first time more often. The same drivers will also be leading to further automation and improvements in the development and delivery of the IT solutions themselves enabling

IT to reengage with business in ways that have so far not been possible. Having been through a phase of introducing prescriptive and rigorous process to systems integration, many organisations are already challenging this route by rejecting waterfall methods in favour of rapid application development and more responsive project management methods; this in turn seems to be appropriate in a world where products have ever-shorter lifecycles.

From the above we can see that evolution takes place because the technology changes and new solutions emerge. With each new product comes a new support requirement and as a new business process is supported so the service requirement changes. Thus there is a constantly changing mix of the product and service components being demanded of the services provider. It is interesting to reflect upon where we have come from and where we are headed. Arguably in the early days we had a large central resource and we grappled with simple technology that required bespoke application solutions, high-volume manual data entry and constant operator attention: the service component was thus very large. Later, as networked desktop systems and packaged (even shrink-wrapped) solutions emerged to be integrated with legacy or industry specific solutions, the servicing element reduced significantly for those businesses that were able to take advantage of the changes. There are many businesses that have subsequently gone down the route of heavy customisation; indeed some high-end commercial enterprise resource management solutions require this. We also know that it is easy to introduce services that demand a high management overhead and the business also has a greater expectation in terms of what the service provider should be delivering. What we are now seeing as a trend is a move towards product as a service and service 'productisation'. This means that probably for the first time since the early days of commercial data processing we are finding that the requirement for the service component is actually growing and new skills are required. This is illustrated in Figure 1.3. This picture is constantly evolving and so we must consider what methods and standards we are using and what situation they were designed for. It would be inappropriate to take methods or standards designed for a 'networked IT and packaged solutions' situation and apply them to a situation requiring greater product and service elements without considering the consequences. As well as the appropriate methods and standards we need to reflect on how we might detect that a change in needs is emerging and that these needs are being satisfied. What should be clear now is that the approach must not just consider IT but the whole business; the approach must be business-focused.

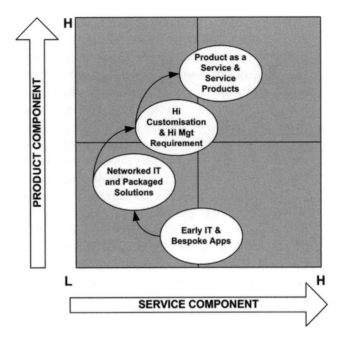

FIGURE 1.3   *Trends in the mix of product and service components*

What Figure 1.3 illustrates is that over time the business requires varying amounts of product and service component to satisfy its needs and that it becomes increasingly difficult for the business to separate one from the other. From a management point of view the two components must in future be delivered in a coordinated way in order to be sure of meeting the needs of the business. Throughout this book we refer to both products and services but where this distinction is not made (either in the text or in diagrams) the reader must assume that the term 'service' also embraces the product component.

A business will find creative ways of satisfying need. What emerges is a complex relationship between organisations, people, process, knowledge and technology (in the form of product and service components). This is complex and adaptive in that it is constantly evolving according to the needs of the business and the range of possible solutions available. We need ways to understand this in order to be able to intervene and improve it. Rather than just focusing on how the technological components are delivered, we also need the tools to look at the requirement gaps that the business might have and their experiences of the how services are currently being provided. We introduce a new service excellence model to help us to understand the nature of any requirement gap, a service engine concept to enable us to assess and improve the total business experience and a new strategy framework to get an understanding of the business model and how IT supports it.

As for the long term, in the service management arena the IT maturity models have been around for a long time. They talk about the ultimate state of maturity as being 'business-driven' but this is then either not defined or is expressed in terms of the current delivery technologies. If instead of taking an IT-focused approach to defining 'business-driven' we take a business-focused approach, then we can begin to consider how a business-driven maturity model might look. Whatever happens, IT will become more embedded in business processes and at some point we may lose the distinction between IT as the provider and the business as the client, customer or user: the two will become one and the same. Yet even when we reach this state we will still need to make an assessment of how well the business needs are being addressed by technology, how well the service compares with the ideal, what can be done to improve the situation, the business case for change, the risks associated with change, the dependencies and how quickly the improvements can be introduced. To help with the way we think about the business and IT in the long term we also introduce a new maturity model.

'Business-focused IT' will thus attempt to provide some answers in these areas. In doing so the intention is to avoid the pitfalls of assuming that technology will look the same in the future. We hope that this book will still have relevance 10 or even 20 years hence and that there is no change in how we make these assessments, just shifts in the actual technology being deployed, delivery methods, the international standards that apply and the nature of the business that IT is servicing. It is our intention that the ideas offered here are not limited to the technology or methodology of the day but a serious attempt to redefine the way in which we assess and so improve the IT services being provided and to provide some insight into the next stages of IT maturity.

MAKING THE CHANGE

Delivery methods reflect the technology, methodology and solutions of the day. If we are to assess an IT service we must look at all aspects and consider them not just from the IT perspective (e.g. the extent to which we comply with a particular process or our ability to implement a particular technology) but from the perspective of business stakeholders (i.e. the extent to which we have achieved what we set out to achieve). We must see a shift then from process to outcome: from how to what.

If IT is to respond to improve outcome it must also be central to the business and close enough to be seen to be relevant. IT must also be agile; it must rapidly develop alliances with experts in any technology which might emerge as being key to the business. Some may trust this to an outsourced service provider or other third party whilst others will prefer that these relationships be managed directly rather than indirectly. Finally IT must be constantly aware of the needs of the business and the market in which the business operates. How IT positions itself relative to the business is very important. This might sound obvious and yet many chief information officers (CIOs) will be uncomfortable with these concepts. According to a Harvey Nash survey, 83% of CIOs questioned recognised that building and maintaining relationships with the business is very important but only 18% believed that their team is excellent at doing it (Harvey Nash 2007). This is lower than the response to the same question the previous year. These people are not short of IT skills but are short of the management skills to adequately develop, build and maintain relationships, yet these are basic skills for most business managers. Most IT service providers make basic mistakes in terms of how they are positioned relative to the business and thereafter everything else becomes difficult.

Ries and Trout (2001) define positioning as how we differentiate our brand in the minds of our customers and prospects. Positioning was known about as long ago as 1969 and today it is used by organisations of all kinds, including political parties. Ries and Trout go on to say that positioning is not what we do to our product or service, it is what we do to the mind of our prospect. Ignore this concept and we leave our prospects to decide for themselves how they would wish to position our organisation, our products, our services and us. The positioning that is to be used must always be plausible to the market and sustainable by the organisation over the long term. This aspect of positioning will be unique to our organisation in terms of where we are now, where we are headed, our skill sets, our major challenges etc. This is not a book about positioning but you will discover after reading it that all services providers will have to address this fundamentally in order to be capable of improving service experience.

We turn now to attitude. This is an aspect of behaviour that also influences what people are thinking about product and service providers. Whilst positioning is unique to each IT organisation, we believe that the need to have the right attitude is common to all. Many would say that this is an era of attitude, where attitude is king. To stand out as individuals we are expected to have attitude. Attitude can have negative connotations associated with arrogance; in this context it is actually more about being noticed. We get noticed by being in the right place at the right time and by standing out from the crowd.

So summarising then, for IT to be noticed it must have attitude, but for IT to be asked to contribute will show that it is essential for it to be seen to be:

- relevant;
- agile;
- aware.

Let us look at how this works in business generally.

Back in 1982, Whitbread rapidly responded (agility) to a lacklustre UK first product launch of Stella Artois (awareness) and quickly repositioned it as a premium (and higher priced) UK brand marketed to the younger sector (relevance). The strategy was reinforced with the slogan 'reassuringly expensive'. This is often quoted amongst marketers as one of the most brilliant repositioning achievements of all time for a consumer brand. Times change and 25 years later, in 2007, the brewer InBev has decided to ask its advertising agency to again reposition the brand in order to distance it from the current culture of binge drinking amongst young people (awareness) and hopefully once more reinvigorate sales.

IBM fiddled whilst its computer manufacturing business dwindled (initial lack of awareness) but successfully reinvented itself (requiring significant agility) as a major services provider (regained market relevance).

In 1991 Gerald Ratner joked candidly (unaware of the impact it would have) and publicly about the quality of his company's products to an audience of Institute of Directors members (something here about relevance) and lost his jewellery business. At the time, Ratners was the world's biggest jewellery chain.

Marks & Spencer's sales had been in decline (aware but it lacked the agility to make its products relevant to a younger age group). It took a new management team, major store refurbishments (renewed agility) and new product lines (regaining relevance) to turn the corner.

If an IT service provider needs to bring about a major turnaround in performance it must also exploit relevance, agility and awareness.

Relevance

IT people are rational, analytical and logical. We have to be in order to make sense of complex business rules so that they can be codified into business and IT systems. Our preference is sometimes to deal with the technology rather than the people in the business. When dealing with people it is usually in the context of processes or technology rather than the less tangible aspects of business. Many consultancies have chanted the mantra of 'people, process and technology': this is a crass over-simplification of the role of IT in the digital era. We should not be surprised when a proposition that is based upon such a limited view of the role of IT fails. At the other extreme, some systems integrators have very complex approaches characterised by multi-page schematic diagrams and a methodology that runs into many volumes (requiring several metres of shelf space) which are also failing the client. Both the over-simplicity on the one hand and the over-complexity on the other are seen to be unhelpful by business. An IT focus, regardless of how it manifests itself, is just seen to be irrelevant.

'Business-focused IT' is about making sure that IT is seen to be relevant to the business. We can develop a generic positioning strategy that is relevant to all IT services organisations. Technology must not only be aligned with people and processes but with the business plan, suppliers, the market and the resources of the business (by driving efficiency and effectiveness). This is the context for IT; we must always position IT as being central to any modern business. IT is not a background activity but a key enabler or even a differentiator (see Figure 1.4).

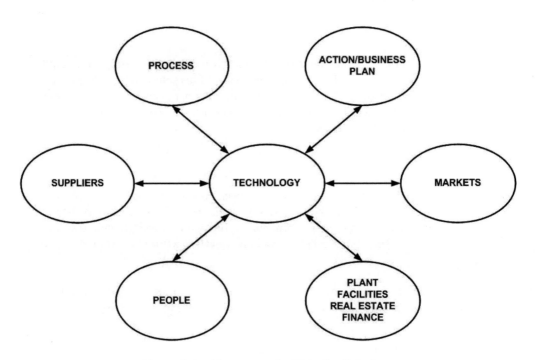

FIGURE 1.4   *The context for IT in the digital era*

Most businesses have a strategy, business plan and even a series of action plans including change programmes. Sometimes the plans are implicit rather than explicit; they may be understood by the board of directors but not always communicated effectively to all stakeholders. If the IT brand is in good health, the business will recognise the benefits of involving IT at an early stage. The business will be seeking to realign IT with where it is headed and looking to find out how IT can be exploited to enable the business to achieve success more quickly or in ways that it had not already considered. Even if IT is not yet at the centre of the business, IT must always be part of this planning process. It is inconceivable that modern businesses can achieve their goals without a major contribution from IT. The fact is that many companies do not feel the need to involve IT in this planning; it is no coincidence that the board level CIO is still relatively rare and IT literate business directors even rarer.

The completed business or action plan is sometimes the start point for IT strategy. Provided that the business is clear in terms of what it wishes to achieve, IT can work with the management team to understand what capabilities need to be brought to bear upon the problem, what technologies need to be deployed and how much should be spent now and over the next few months or years. If the business or action plan is at all unclear, IT must work with the business to ensure that everyone understands what they need to do to deliver the plan and to clearly define the IT requirement.

Let us consider the other aspects of the context: supply chain, markets, process, people and the resources that will be needed to execute the plan (plant, facilities, real estate and finance).

The supply chain is the source of all raw materials and supplier services. Failure to establish strong links with suppliers to the business leads to higher than necessary costs as well as purchasing, stock holding, quality and lead time issues. If higher costs are not incurred directly they will be incurred by the supplier and passed on. IT is now essential for managing an effective supply chain in all industry sectors and it also extends reach (i.e. manufacturing and transportation can be managed across all continents).

The market is the object of commercial success; 'not for profit' and public sector organisations have proxies for this focus along the lines that the beneficiary of the service will be the judge of its value. Commercial success, or its proxy, is achieved through better sales and service. The business landscape is changing and companies must do what they can to secure and develop their market. IT is not just a key enabler and IT people must know enough about the market to develop effective business solutions.

Plant, facilities, real estate and finance are the resources referred to by economists that will be used to generate more wealth through the value added by the business. As well as adding value and opportunities for competitive advantage, IT investment is enabling costs to be driven out of businesses through more efficient processes, freeing up traditional assets and enabling businesses to be created at minimum cost. Sometimes we need to release money tied up in traditional assets and we in IT should be proficient at making this happen if this will help to fund the IT investment.

Processes are being underpinned with technology so that they are as efficient and as effective as possible. Organisations often seek to ensure that processes reflect best practice, that they are implemented in a uniform and consistent manner throughout the world and that they can easily and quickly be updated everywhere when necessary. Technologies are emerging that simplify both the underpinning and the change processes.

People are the users of IT and IT-enabled processes. Almost 100% of white-collar workers have the use of at least one PC and the percentage is growing amongst blue-collar workers. Processors can take different forms and can be embedded in devices, appliances, plant and machinery. The convergence of technologies brings more processes within the scope of IT and more people into contact with IT. IT people need to be able to communicate with all of them.

IT now supports or underpins almost all aspects of business but even so the IT budget these days can still be a very small percentage of the total cost of running a business; too small to necessarily convince chief executive officers (CEOs) that IT is central to the business or that IT should have a seat at the boardroom table. The impact of IT on any business, however, is without question the greatest of all of the management disciplines: whether we consider efficiency, effectiveness or return on investment (ROI), the deployment of IT will be of critical importance. What needs to be spent on IT and its impact will depend upon where the business is now and where it is headed, the current status of IT, the supporting IT strategy, planned change programmes and IT service level requirements. These are critical areas for any business and require a relevant and business-focused approach.

Agility

Agility takes many forms. When we talk about agility we may be referring to speed to market, adaptability to new competitive strategies, responsiveness to change etc. All of these are desirable qualities but in the fast-moving technology sector, agility is driven by innovation and flexibility.

At the start of the digital era, most IT organisations were seen to be at the leading edge and they attracted innovative and energetic people who seemed to be able to do everything. Today by contrast we often see IT organisations that have become fixed in the ways they view the business, the IT opportunity, their methods and their own roles. This is not so much a reflection on today's people as on the range of different skills that are required and the bureaucracy that has grown up around the discipline as it has matured. In the IT sector we know that, from our own research, innovation and flexibility can be recreated by introducing a more dynamic IT organisation and supply strategy.

Imagine the IT demand and supply cycles. A customer organisation will develop business strategy, define IT requirements, deliver change and review progress. The supply industry will consider the customer business requirement, develop a proposal, manage resource (to deliver change to the customer business), reassess what business it is in, and develop a new

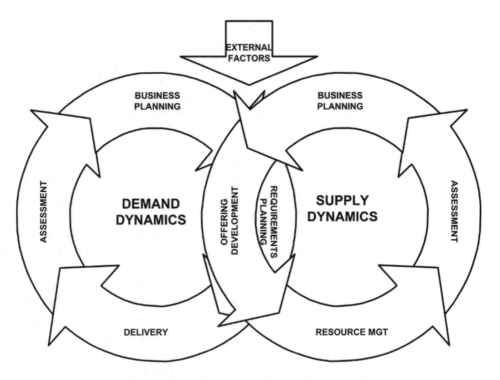

FIGURE 1.5 *Dynamics of demand and supply*

offering based on the skills recently acquired, the market etc. Interfering with the natural processes are the external factors such as the political, fiscal, environmental, sociological and technological influences (PFEST) which will encourage or discourage investment; these are particularly key at the time the strategy of both the customer and the supplier organisations are being reviewed and updated. This can be generalised to apply to any business-to-business relationship and we refer to this as the business-to-business dynamics of demand and supply (see Figure 1.5).

Either the demand or the supply cycle can dominate. A business can define its requirements and test these against the market to see who can deliver; alternatively a supplier can develop a solution and market this to the prospective clients who are most likely to benefit from the technology (segmentation). Whichever way this comes about the cycles will develop post delivery and result in new business strategies based upon the most recent experience and the latest PFEST climate. The dynamics can be changed by the supplier becoming proactive and helping to define the requirement thus speeding up the development of the offering.

The potential for innovation is clearly at its greatest at the point where business requirements and the offerings from the market come together, that is, where the demand and supply cycles overlap. Intuitively we must all recognise this as being the case. By stimulating demand and supply relationships we can create more innovation. More competition and more suppliers also create organisational flexibility because businesses do not have to employ so many specialists on a permanent basis; they just hire the specialists when required. Much better then to encourage appropriate relationships with a range of suppliers and so provide access to the right skills in a timely manner as and when needed, thereby reducing time to market whilst gaining greater innovation and flexibility.

Awareness

If we have positioned IT correctly and it is seen to be relevant and have agility, then we must now ensure that the newfound innovation and flexibility is channelled in the right way. Most IT people are aware of technology but this can only benefit the business if IT is fully aware of the needs of the stakeholder community. We must understand who the stakeholders are, what their needs are and in what ways IT can contribute to the success of the venture. This involves being business savvy.

When marketing people look at a market, they are unlikely to see it as being homogenous but rather as being comprised of a number of different segments with different characteristics and needs. We must regard the stakeholder community in the same way and cater for the needs of these different groups and so ensure that they in turn make their maximum contribution to the success of our service, programme or assignment.

If we are to learn from the extreme if simplistic case of Gerald Ratner, we must ensure that we are aware of our audience (or stakeholders), aware of their interests and aware that there may be serious consequences of getting our communications with them wrong. Whilst the consequences of inappropriate communication can be immediate, the consequences of poor or inadequate communication develop over a considerable period but are just as catastrophic. Either way the effect is one of disenfranchisement. There is a simple framework that we can use to make us think about how well communications are being managed as illustrated in Figure 1.6.

We identify the various stakeholder groups that are relevant to our business (these can sometimes be many in number and more diverse than those illustrated). Do not forget to include the IT organisation itself and its various specialist groups if this is relevant. We then assess how effectively IT and IT management communicates with each group of stakeholders. Do we have a two-way dialogue with each group and do we understand their needs and opinions? If you are a business manager consider the quality of the communication between your IT service provider and each part of your business. Answering this requires honesty because what one party sees as a meaningful relationship the other can view as lacking in substance. This process requires inputs from a generous sample of each of the stakeholder groups.

This is the first of many radar diagrams we use to express various kinds of assessment. None are absolute measures. The upper or 'Ideal' is an expression of what is needed and it is always expressed as 100%.

The lower 'Assessment' is an estimate of how close to the ideal we rate (in this case) the quality of the dialogue we have with the stakeholders at each point on the diagram. So in the example in Figure 1.6 we have rated the communications we have with the parent company as being very poor (30%), whilst that with Business Group G is rated close to ideal (90%). In fact in terms of the absolute amounts of communication this may be higher in the case of the parent company but the assessment is reflecting the quality of that dialogue compared with what everyone thinks is needed. Hence in this example there is likely to be a lack of awareness of the requirements or intentions of the parent company.

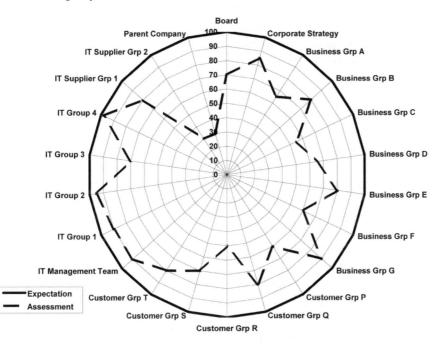

FIGURE 1.6   *Assessing stakeholder communications*

Chart this as we have done, see where your shortfalls lie, consider the consequences and consider what might be done to improve the situation. Date the chart, develop a plan of action and look at it again in 90 days to see if there have been any improvements. If this is something that you find useful it is a good idea to set quality standards for your scoring so that the measures can be a little more objective and the standards reflect your personal targets for a relationship. So for example 10% may indicate that there is only occasional dialogue and then only if initiated by the IT service provider whereas 90% may represent a situation where there are weekly two-way briefings and regular phone calls between meetings to discuss business/IT related opportunities/requirements and where business and IT planning is totally integrated.

Davidson (2002) says that the new challenge is that of gaining commitment from all stakeholders. He ranks stakeholders in importance; his view is that in companies the finance provider is the most important stakeholder but in 'not for profit' organisations it is the customer. He does acknowledge however that the customer will become the dominant stakeholder for most organisations over the coming years. The framework in Figure 1.6 does not show which stakeholders are the most important at any point in time, just the adequacy of the communication. Thus if a stakeholder rises in importance we may choose to reassess the adequacy of current levels of communication. It is through communication that we are able to manage and align stakeholders. Some organisations have complex stakeholder relationships where needs often conflict and in order to be seen to be succeeding we have to devise ways in which we can retain the support of all or most of them.

Having mapped the adequacy of our communications with our stakeholders we have to consider what actions are necessary. Why did we mark our awareness low? Was this because we do not understand their needs, because we have not had the opportunity to talk about how we can meet their needs or has some incident in the past created a situation where relationships are soured and is preventing any progress being made? We have to consider what the consequences might be if the stakeholder group withdrew their support for our organisation or our programme. Regardless of the cause of the difficulty the organisation must find ways to improve the amount and the quality of the communication with all relevant stakeholder groups. This might involve being invited to participate in existing divisional, departmental and functional planning or change programme meetings. It might involve initiating meetings or setting up regular opportunities to share views on the market. Having identified the problem it can be addressed. What frequently goes wrong is that these groups are either never identified as critical stakeholders or the level of communication with them is never identified as being unsatisfactory or inadequate. Better communication always leads to a closer relationship, more work and more successful projects.

2 Service Excellence

Businesses need to establish the macro-level performance of departments, key suppliers and service providers. Traditionally we have tried to measure contribution but in the case of an IT service provider this can be complex. For an IT-driven change programme it is easier perhaps to look at the financial ROI. Perhaps IT service can be measured in terms of the efficient use of capital equipment, such as utilisation or performance metrics such as 'availability'. Perhaps we can use comparisons or benchmark metrics by looking at how we compare in expenditure and performance terms with peer organisations. Perhaps we can use some form of customer satisfaction survey. Whatever benchmark or survey method is used it is not uncommon for the business customers of these organisations to appear to be highly satisfied according to the survey whilst privately expressing dissatisfaction with the service they experience. The service providers to these businesses are the 'trophy organisations' referred to in the introduction, proudly displaying their industry awards for customer service but who still have dissatisfied customers.

So what is happening? The simple truth is that whilst these metrics, benchmarks and surveys may give us an idea of some aspects of performance they are often not in themselves sufficient to uncover the 'word on the street', that is they often do not tell us how well we are addressing business needs, what stakeholders are thinking and what we must do to improve the situation. There is evidence that we ask questions in the surveys that we know will receive good ratings so reinforcing the good aspects of performance and not revealing where and how we might improve (i.e. they are typically incomplete and biased in favour of what we already know we do well). They are typically focused upon physical and transactional encounters rather than interactional encounters (Horovitz 2000), not to mention emotional encounters. This means that our techniques are likely to be incomplete and unhelpful when change is taking place (i.e. most of the time).

MIND THE GAP

There has always been a divide between those who understand the technology of business and those who run businesses; anyone that spends any time at the cusp of the two will know how acute this can be. This is not to say that IT people are not trying: almost since the digital era began IT people have endeavoured to deliver more capability and ever better service levels, but ask the average business manager about IT and there will often be a degree of cynicism and dissatisfaction. If we can understand the reasons for this 'perception gap' and close it then IT service providers could maximise levels of service in every aspect of their interaction with their business community.

Reasons for the perception gap

Most IT service providers have an average delivery record but business perceptions are much worse. As we discussed in the introduction, in spite of the many methods and international standards we are using, if we are still hitting the same project failure rates that we were hitting 20 years ago then we have to ask questions about these methods and standards. In some organisations we have reached the stage where it is better to be seen to comply with the methods, standards or processes than to succeed, in other words we are witnessing the triumph of process over outcome. This is particularly true in risk-averse organisations which have a particular reliance upon methods, standards, procedures and guidelines. It is particularly evident where there is a strong blame culture, poor training and poor motivation.

We must challenge a method or approach that is based upon best practice and which has become some kind of standard if we think it is disconnected from the business, is inappropriately implemented, where it does not fit with the culture of the business or where it is incomplete or inconsistent. In other words, where the method or approach is not business-focused.

Another reason for the perception gap is the questionnaire or benchmark. Many business people have been around the block a few times and will know that questionnaires are often designed to make the organisation look good. This can be achieved simply by the choice of question, the phrasing of the question and the choice of answers offered. In the case of benchmarks, the choice of the comparison company is clearly key together with the degree of openness of the results.

Finally, as product and business lifecycles have become shorter and regulation and compliance are becoming more burdensome, IT has become more critical to the business. Any perception gap creates greater tensions between the business and its IT service provider which, if left unchecked, can provoke a tough response from the business: most outsourcing decisions and changes of supplier are taken in a belief that some kind of gap will be closed.

Process and outcome

We usually introduce new processes in order to achieve predictable outcomes and performance and business life would be great if we could guarantee the relationship between process and outcome. The benefits of a formalised process are that we can introduce consistency by replicating performance and replicate improvement when ways of reducing time or cost or increasing quality are discovered. A formalised process also enables us to communicate better between organisations by introducing common terminology, identifying process interfaces, establishing norms etc. In general the benefit is that processes reflect best practice and so by adopting them we are able to compete more effectively. By prescribing process and through the introduction of automation we are also able to de-skill or downsize and so further reduce costs.

The downside is that methods, if they are to be formally adopted by government agencies and standards bodies, can take time to develop and time to agree. As a result they can often be behind the curve, particularly during periods of technological or process change; collective thinking and insight has moved on but the standard perpetuates the old process. It can become increasingly difficult for an organisation to get ahead of the curve if standards and methods are embedded in process. As a result it would be foolish for an organisation to measure performance against the process unless it is just looking for accreditation but many organisations, especially risk-averse organisations, do just this. As well as possibly being behind the curve, methods often use different terminology and even different philosophies thus making it difficult when trying to comply with more than one standard, for example many organisations use project templates rather than release management processes (as in ITIL and ISO/IEC 20000). Many organisations use project management methods as well as release management methods and unfortunately the terminology is different. The author has seen an inappropriate project template being used for a major healthcare programme that resulted in as many as 400 processes that delivered no value whatsoever but which were merely there to satisfy a standard whereas only 70 processes were required to deliver the whole programme. More process than is necessary does not normally reduce risk: it increases it. We must instead measure our performance against outcomes because these will always be business-focused. By formalising the methods used we can repeat successes and identify what further improvements in outcome can be introduced.

No process can deliver the required outcome without adequate controls. Whether we are looking at project delivery or service delivery we need controls on the process and yet many methods and standards either do not attempt to suggest what these might be or they are defined inadequately. What often emerges is an uncontrollable process that will yield unpredictable outcomes. Mostly success has more to do with the choice of control than choice of process because to obtain the result we have been able to be resourceful about how we did things (although controls with no process would not be helpful).

Process and culture

When we are considering the introduction of process, it is a good idea to give some thought as to how this will fit with the corporate culture. There have been many attempts to characterise organisational culture but it is interesting to look at these from the point of view of how likely some of these organisations are to adapt to structured methods. In almost every case, we are introducing structure in order to make our life in IT easier when introducing complex change but it is clear that this is not always acceptable to the business. If a process helps, that is great; if it does not, let us get rid of the bureaucracy and the cost. Later, in the section covering people, organisation and governance, we look at corporate culture in more detail, but for now accept that many businesses may have a culture that is unsuited to a highly structured approach.

Empirically we can observe this in our daily working lives and yet methodologies and practitioners alike almost totally ignore this. Many organisations will go along with rational and structured approaches in the case of IT because they often do not understand it and have bought into a process on the basis that it is supposed to be best practice. Clues as to the underlying culture of a business can be found by observing its behaviour in different situations. Look at how decisions concerning the core business are taken compared with IT investment decisions and try to work out what is happening and how the culture can be adapted to IT.

Sometimes we see the IT service provider itself rebel against excessive process. In a way the current move to 'agile' is a kickback against the waterfall methods and the bureaucracy that has grown up around them. Some of us are old enough to remember that before the rise of structured methods, agile was the normal way. We can consider that agile is merely an outcome-focused approach to software development.

The implications of adopting a business focus

We must continue to retain our internal success criteria but we must recognise this as micro-management. In addition we must introduce measures on outcomes that are meaningful to the business. We must also develop a much better understanding of how people perceive our overall performance. We need to understand how our performance is perceived by all stakeholders at all levels: by business managers, by the users of the systems and services, by customers of the business where our applications and services reach out to them (and perhaps even if they do not but should do so), the IT people (because they are often aware of their own shortcomings and we need to understand both cause and effect), suppliers to both the business and to the IT services provider and maybe other key stakeholders. In this way we build a more complete (a 360°) picture of our performance. To be business-focused we must always look at our performance through the eyes of others.

Analysts have often tried to understand how high-performing businesses operate and then try to systematise best practice in order to repeat the success. Unfortunately it cannot always be interpreted so easily and does not translate well for others to apply. We refer to high-performing businesses as 'world class' but the term itself is imprecise. We may be talking about meeting national and international standards that may be relevant in our market place. We may be adding low cost and delivery on time to the mix as suggested by Morton (1994). Maybe we should be taking away rather than combining as suggested by Treacy and Wiersema (1995) and so choosing between operational excellence, product leadership and customer intimacy (i.e. we choose how we wish to be seen to be world class). Maybe there is a business model that will help us to get a better understanding. Do we care? Many organisations that have claimed to be world class have long gone, many others are clearly not, and yet the expression still has a meaning to many businesses and to many potential buyers of our products and services.

As our services address more business needs and we measure our performance against business criteria, we become more business-focused and we begin to improve satisfaction ratings. As well as needing new measures we must become more comfortable with subjective measures and we need to develop the tools and mindset (attitude) to become business-focused. By being business-focused we improve satisfaction ratings and through continuous improvement processes we achieve greater service excellence.

We need new, more business-focused, ways to look at both the bigger picture and the detailed aspects of any service, not just complex aspects such as IT. We need to better understand the macro- and micro-aspects of service as it is being experienced by the business. It is obvious to most business people now that there is a need to comprehensively understand how a service provider can achieve service excellence and that this is key to achieving greater business success.

DEFINING SERVICE EXCELLENCE

Our first consideration should perhaps be the European Foundation for Quality Management (EFQM) model. This was produced in 1992 originally as the framework for the UK Excellence Award. It is used to assess an organisation's progress towards excellence and the percentages are based on European averages. It consists of nine criteria: leadership, people, policy and strategy, processes, people results, customer results, society results and key performance results. It suggests that processes (14%) are almost as important as key performance (business) results (15%). This was the real beginning of the significance of process. It also lists leadership, people management, policy and strategy and resources as key enablers and recognises that people satisfaction, customer satisfaction and impact on society are all valid results. Even if this has been useful in the past, it is a generalised business model and so a drive for service excellence combined with a need for more importance to be given to results or outcome rather than approach suggests that the EFQM model on its own will no longer be sufficient.

Parasuraman et al. (1985) devised the service quality model (SQM). This was a model that highlighted the gaps between consumers of service and service providers. A major conclusion from the research was that many discrepancies exist between perceptions of service quality and the tasks associated with the service delivery to customers. These gaps can be major hurdles in attempting to deliver a service which consumers would perceive as being of high quality. A further conclusion from this work was that there was an absence of a wholehearted management commitment to service quality. The model is illustrated in Figure 2.1.

The SQM usefully differentiates between needs, expectation, perception, service delivery, service specification and personal needs. As the model describes a business-to-consumer service, it should not be surprising to find that when used to assess a business-to-business service the model is lacking in a number of areas. Also, because of the lack of detail relating to the more complex business-to-business environment there is little separation of the possibilities of the causes of dissatisfaction and so there is a diminished possibility of achieving performance improvement. The model describes an arms-length service culture based upon assumptions of needs with no real-time feedback of performance. Perhaps the greatest giveaway as to its origin is the limited range of external influences and those that do exist drive expectation and not needs. We can assume that this model was well conceived for its day but it describes a world in which things happen because in a business-to-consumer world there is always an assumption about need and that ultimately this is what has to be tested against consumer demand. The concepts may still be sound today in a consumer market but it was certainly never intended to model something as complex as a business-to-business service or IT service provision. Trying to use the model however opened up a new avenue of thought and some new research and new ideas.

Milner (1995) was also looking at the business-to-consumer sectors when he talked about perspectives and constraints: the relationship between the business environment, resources and expectations. He suggested that whichever of the three perspectives is adopted, the other two will then act as constraints. Suppose for example that a business adopts an environment-based perspective. Its ability to seek out and pursue opportunities in the external environment will be limited by its resources on the one hand and by the expectations and power of people on the other. Similarly an expectations-based strategy will be limited by the business environment and resources. Business environment, resources and expectation are also significant in terms of business-to-business services.

Bringing these various ideas together and setting them into the more complex business-to-business context we then have the concept of the

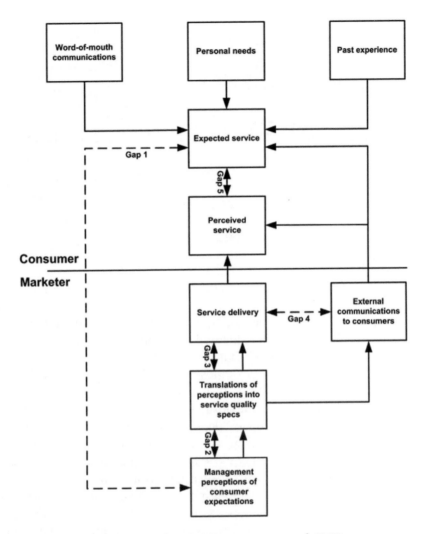

FIGURE 2.1   *The SQM (Parasuraman et al. 1985)*

ITDYNAMICS™ service excellence model (Figure 2.2). We can use this to examine the adequacy of our service from a business perspective and also use it to help us to understand how a service might evolve in the future with a suggestion for a new maturity model.

Today wherever we look we observe a world in which we all seek instant gratification. Governments are measured based on their performance during four or five year terms, if not on weekly opinion surveys. Consumers want to buy immediately and have access to instant credit. Populations will migrate rather than try to improve the economy of their own territory or their personal circumstances locally. Stock markets expect ever-improving returns. Products have ever-shorter lifecycles.

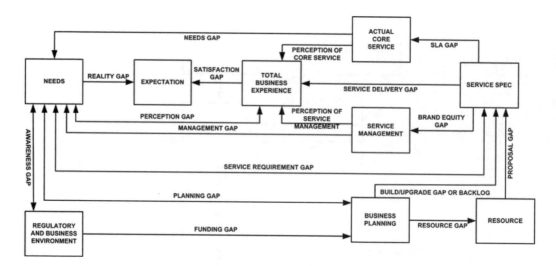

FIGURE 2.2   *The ITDYNAMICS™ service excellence model*

IT is in turn becoming more intimately related to business. Technology is becoming embedded within many processes and even in product. The business model that emerges from these changes is going to look very different. We start to lose the stark separation we see in the SQM of 1985 between supply and demand: needs will be based on more immediate things such as the business and competitive environment; we are going to see strong feedback loops to understand how investments in the service are being received using continuous improvements such as those expressed by Deming, ISO/IEC 20000 and Six Sigma; there will be a tighter coupling of the relationships between the business and the service provider through the business planning process. Service excellence will be judged by the business based on its experience of using the service. Service will be supported by process based on methods and standards but any shortfall in performance to the business will be identified as a gap. By identifying the nature of these gaps and closing them we will be able to raise levels of business satisfaction and get closer to meeting the business need.

We no longer assume that satisfaction and perception gaps will be based on a simple comparison of how well the IT services supplier meets the service-level agreement (SLA) but on how closely the customer's total business experience matches business needs. This leads us to define a new model based on the quest for service excellence. By understanding and minimising each gap the service provider brings what is delivered closer to these needs. By shortening lead times the service provider responds more quickly to changing needs. The ITDYNAMICS™ service excellence model defines a hierarchy of gaps which can help us to understand the cause and effect of any weakness of a service.

The primary gap expressed in this model is that between the needs and the service spec and we call it the service requirement gap.

Above this line we break out the components of service delivery and below the components of service planning. Today the service planning gaps will probably not be the responsibility of the service provider, but every service provider should be aware of all gaps, the reasons for their existence and be prepared to provide the business with whatever help may be needed to close them. It is worth noting that any aspect of service planning that is not adequately being addressed will ultimately give rise to the perception of a gap somewhere in the service delivery zone which is always seen to be the responsibility of the service provider. The service planning zone and service delivery zone of the model are illustrated more clearly in Figure 2.3 where they are separated by the dotted line. The service planning zone can be separated into those gaps that arise from business planning (or a lack of it) and those that arise from ordering changes to the service specification.

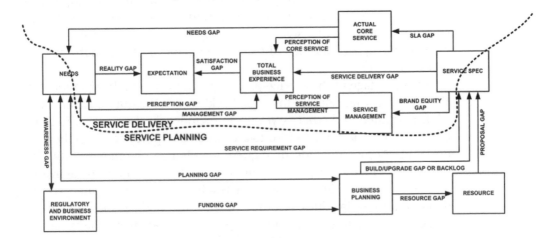

FIGURE 2.3 *The planning and delivery zones of the service excellence model*

A planning gap arises where there is no worthwhile investment portfolio (from a business perspective) or sales pipeline (from a service provider perspective). The gap exists where a requirement has either not been identified or was not submitted for funding in any kind of business planning process. This may be a consequence of insufficient business planning or it could be a conscious decision not to invest at this point in time based on some well-considered rationale. Breaking this down further there is the possibility of an awareness gap or a funding gap. An awareness gap can arise because a business is unaware of the external drivers for change, for example if there is a failure by the business to fully understand the business environment, if the business fails to understand how competitors are exploiting technology or if a business fails to appreciate the changes taking place in the regulatory environment in that business sector. An appropriate remedy for the service organisation would be to regularly brief the business using relevant intelligence for that sector. For this to be effective the intelligence must be from reliable and reputable sources, it must be delivered to the right people and it must be delivered with additional information that will answer the predictable questions that will follow. The frequency of briefings will depend upon the dynamics of the sector. The business leaders will need to know what can be done to catch up or gain advantage, how much that is likely to cost and when it can be delivered. Ballpark estimates at this stage are fine. The ideal remedy for the services organisation is to be sufficiently close to the business to be aware of the reason for any gaps and to intervene if there is a good reason to do so. A funding gap arises where either a requirement exists but may not be submitted to the business planning process in the belief that it may not be affordable or where the business is prepared to forgo the benefits of the investment. A remedy should be pursued if the IT service organisation believes that the funding gap is based on incorrect or insufficient information (e.g. where the potential solution is not as expensive as the business thinks or where a signifi-cant proportion of the benefits could be achieved for a more modest investment etc.).

The final stage of the service planning zone is the build/upgrade gap. This is sometimes referred to as the backlog. It is the difference between what is funded and what is yet to be included in the service. It could be some new hardware or software purchase, product or application development, an upgrade or request for change or other facility. The remedy is to manage expectation about what can reasonably be delivered and by when. It will increase as a result of an unanticipated rise in demand for new facilities, resource constraints, inefficiencies in delivery, or a poor supply strategy. The build/upgrade gap can further be expanded to identify any resource gap or proposal gap.

Business planning (and so business service planning) is influenced by a complex set of values based on the business experience of receiving the service. This will inevitably influence a business' propensity to invest further in the service. This being the case we must look at the service delivery zone of the service excellence model in greater depth.

The service delivery zone breaks down the service requirement gap from a delivery perspective. At the heart of the service delivery zone is something that we refer to as the 'total business experience'. This concept is central to business-focused IT. The total business experience is the output from the 'service engine'. It is what the business experiences in terms of what is delivered, some of which can be measured quantitatively and some of which will be measured qualitatively but which will nevertheless make up the total picture of how a business might describe what it is getting from a service provider. The shortfall between the total business experience and the (business) needs is called the perception gap. We can further break this down to distinguish between the needs and expectation (the reality gap) and the difference between expectation and the total business experience (the satisfaction gap).

When a service provider markets its services it stimulates need. Expectation is need modified by knowledge of the service provider or by the experience of using the service. Most businesses will recognise that they have needs which they know cannot reasonably be met by their service provider. In Parasuraman et al.'s (1985) business-to-consumer SQM the expectation was set by word of mouth and past experience. In the business-to-business service excellence model, expectation could be based upon this and other more numerous sources of information including researched or perceived limitations in capability, for example the technology available to the service provider does not meet all of the needs of the business or perhaps the range of services is limited. Whatever capability is lacking will lower expectation and create a reality gap. The service provider needs to be close to the business in order to be aware of the existence of any reality gap and must find ways in which expectation can be raised, for example by informing the business of actual or new capability (note that this may involve entering into an alliance with another supplier). This is often the opposite of what actually happens. Service providers talk about managing expectation in order that what is delivered more closely meets this lower level of expectation. Managing expectation tends to increase satisfaction (by closing the satisfaction gap) at the expense of widening the reality gap. This merely opens up the possibility of more competition for supply.

The satisfaction gap is what is typically measured by those predictable satisfaction surveys. It is the uninformed view of the difference between what is delivered and the expectation. In an absence of an understanding of the service excellence model, any measure of satisfaction can be misleading.

It is now time to introduce the concept of the service engine (see Figure 2.4). The total business experience is delivered by the service engine and is broken down into two components. The first is the actual core service and the second is service management. Both are based upon the service spec. The general case is true for any service and the model can be used in any sector though the components of the service engine will vary between sectors, particularly the core service components. In the specific case of IT services we have developed an IT service engine which we describe in detail in the next section. By understanding all of the components of a service engine we can identify the strengths and weaknesses of any given service and prescribe a wider range of remedies that will enable us to understand how we might close all gaps and so improve performance.

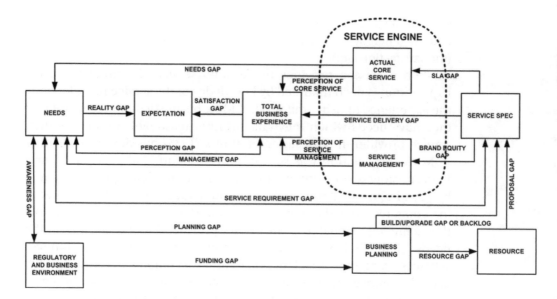

FIGURE 2.4   *The service engine of the service excellence model*

The SLA gap is any shortfall in terms of the core service that was specified or implied by the service spec but not actually delivered and it is generally what is measured by the service provider. Similarly the brand equity gap is the shortfall in terms of service management that was specified or implied by the service spec that is not actually delivered (and it is rarely measured by the service provider). In other words if we can detect any gap we can say that the service engine is deficient when compared with specification. This may be recognised by the business as a service delivery gap without necessarily detecting whether the gap was due to a SLA gap or to a brand equity gap; some prior knowledge of what was in the specification would be required to be able to detect this.

The output from the service engine is what delivers the total business experience. Within this we may separately identify the perception of core service and the perception of service management. These are again the perceptions of most business users who do not define the needs or the service spec but who nevertheless assess the service received as it is delivered, that is in the context of their own needs and experience.

Higher up the business hierarchy any shortfall in output from the service engine will be interpreted as not just a perception gap but also possibly a needs gap. The needs gap is based on the business perception of the adequacy of the core service compared with needs. The management gap is based on the aspects that describe the service and make it accessible at the point of delivery versus the needs. As a service provider we may refer to this latter characteristic as 'brand' but at the point where the service is experienced it is more usually perceived as 'management'.

It is easy to see how a service provider can be monitoring the SLA gap and be blissfully unaware of any service delivery problems. We can see that there could be many reasons why the business might consider that the service is not meeting its needs even when there is a zero SLA gap.

The remedy is for the service provider to invest more in the skills and activities that will identify and address more of the needs. As business managers become more demanding IT service providers need to use a wider range of skills than most IT professionals would expect or would normally use. The deficiencies in service are mostly remedied by resourcing the organisation with the skills needed to deliver all aspects of service in the proportion required to meet the commercial, emotional and functional needs of the business. For example this may be to put greater effort into understanding the needs, finding ways of increasing the value of the solutions deployed, providing an account manager to become the primary interface to a new and critical part of the business or a product manager to explain how a product/service solution can benefit a business and what it takes to deploy it, or even to provide a solution to freeing capital tied up in redundant plant, equipment or real estate as a result of change. The total business experience then is the business or user's perspective of all aspects of the service delivered. The service we are concerned with in this publication is an IT service and we examine the engine that drives this service and its key components in some detail. Other services will have different engines but we can consider the service excellence model to be a generalised concept suited to any product or service and which will handle all complexities.

Many of these gaps can be bridged over time but the longer it takes for the service provider to bridge the gaps the more likely these gaps will become an insurmountable problem in the mind of the business. A service provider can establish a reputation for under-performance or just not being in the market to provide what is needed. In a multi-supplier environment a business will bridge the gaps by speaking to those suppliers perceived as having the required solutions. If this is to be avoided, service providers must understand how well they are performing, understand what the business thinks about them and understand the basis for these opinions. Performance improvement programmes must be based on a broad spectrum of behaviour: just how broad will become clearer later. The service provider must even take responsibility for gaps that appear to lie with the business, or accept the consequences.

ALIGNMENT

Intellectually there are just two approaches to alignment. Mostly the recommended approach is to align IT with the business. Kaplan and Norton (1996) started by introducing the balanced scorecard to provide and measure the operational interpretation of strategy that had a neutral stance toward technology. Their next stage was to introduce strategy maps as a means of creating value from the scorecard using IT to support process (Kaplan and Norton 2004). The latest stage is to talk about alignment, including aligning the IT organisation using a generic IT department strategy template that considers operational excellence through IT solutions, creating and supporting business partnerships by IT becoming a trusted advisor and strategic support to the business through innovative solutions (Kaplan and Norton 2006). Admittedly they acknowledge that IT must contribute to value creation but this can be lost in the general rush to assume that it is the IT that has to be aligned. If this had been the general case over the last 30–40 years then fewer benefits would have been derived from IT than is actually the case. IT realignment projects in major corporations tend to expend at least half of their energy changing the business to better exploit IT. In every case the process has been one of changing the dynamics to create and evaluate opportunities rather than to merely reengineer the architecture or business applications to support a restructured business (although much of this has been undertaken as well). Businesses restructure in order to free themselves up to tackle markets more effectively, either by eliminating overhead costs, by eliminating unnecessary process or by creating new possibilities. They will reengineer the supply chain, better support the business plan and organisational goals, restructure the organisation and make better use of plant, facilities and real estate. In fact this is the context for IT as discussed earlier and so that a context diagram can be used as a generic framework for whatever needs to be considered. This becomes the starting point for better communication between the business and IT and for the realignment of IT. This is further developed under the heading of marketing and communication in the next section.

A second way to approach alignment is to use the ITDYNAMICS™ service excellence model to identify and eliminate gaps, that is we ensure that there is no unintentional service requirement gap arising as a result of service planning or service delivery.

There is a third consideration: we must also ensure that major change programmes also maintain an alignment with the changing needs of the business throughout their life.

The complexities created by inappropriate IT that has not been kept up to date with the needs of the business are difficult to change quickly but with a common purpose and convergent endeavours much can be achieved. What service providers must be capable of doing in these situations is to bring a broad range of skills into play to make sense of the needs of the business and the gaps that can be closed. IT is capable of making a difference – of adding value.

To better understand the range of skills we need in order to make a difference and to have a chance of delivering service excellence we must examine the service engine that both gives rise to the total business experience, and that has the ability to close the gaps of the service excellence model.

3 The Service Engine and the Total Business Experience

We said in the previous section that IT had to take a broader view of the business experience and business needs if it was to successfully eliminate the gaps and drive IT service excellence. Whilst the service excellence model takes a macro-level view we need something that will enable us to take a micro-level view of what IT does. We must understand what aspects of the product or service are valued by the business and the skills that are required to deliver them. We must maximise stakeholder satisfaction by harnessing these in every interaction with the business community. We know that high stakeholder satisfaction cannot usually be achieved by just delivering the basic product or service. We have seen that the service requirement gap is in fact not one simple gap but potentially a complex range of gaps arising for many different reasons that have their origin, not just in IT, but maybe in the business strategy or business planning processes. Nevertheless, the service provider must address these gaps if its reputation is to be protected. Perhaps the service provided lacks commercial confidence or emotional appeal and the service provider needs to learn new skills in order to start adding more value. By looking at the service delivery engine we can establish what is working well and what is not, which skills exist and which need to be improved.

Most IT organisations maintain comprehensive metrics which are typically precise quantitative measurements of activities, events or aspects of service. Within IT there are internal measures of performance and capacity that IT needs in order to be sure that tolerances are not being exceeded within the operational processes. At the business interface the metrics relate to the service delivered (i.e. output) versus the service level that was specified (i.e. the SLA gap). The service excellence model presented above now enables us to recognise that these kinds of service-level metrics represent a very narrow view of the service that the business experiences and that these metrics are therefore, and have always been, insufficient for assessing all aspects of the service provided to a business. Many IT organisations also benchmark their performance with organisations of a similar size or in the same sector: again this is mostly the comparison of core service metrics and most organisations seem to report that their performance compares favourably with that of their peers. As was mentioned earlier, organisations may from time to time undertake customer satisfaction surveys: these measure the satisfaction gap which compares expectation with the total business experience. It typically contains significantly more qualitative data than the core service metrics but questions are often phrased such that they prompt favourable answers and yield high scores: in fact all of these metrics frequently return high scores and consequently provide endorsement to the processes in use.

As we have heard, invariably the customers of these organisations have a different view. Just as we have a better way now of identifying and distinguishing between different types of gap, we also need a better way of assessing the skills required to deliver good service. The approach described here does that and goes a long way towards explaining how seemingly successful services organisations that think they are providing a great service may in fact be perceived differently by their customers.

If we examine the different aspects of customer expectation that the IT organisation should be attempting to satisfy, we can divide these into two groups. The first is concerned with the core product or service and the second satisfies our need to know about the product or service and so shapes our view of the brand and management.

By assessing each of these aspects more fully, we not only build up a picture of what the business is experiencing but also where there are shortfalls in delivery and (unlike the customer satisfaction questionnaires) what the opportunities for improvement might be. It would be naive to believe that the concept of brand equity alone accounts for the perception gap but it can be harnessed to find ways of introducing desirable change. Brand equity is used here as a way of summarising the effectiveness of the less tangible aspects of service allowing us to encompass the broader aspects of stakeholder satisfaction concerned with service management and the image that creates.

Deficiencies in either the core service or brand equity will always yield lower perceptions of satisfaction within the business. Marketers believe that stakeholder experience is not the sum of both but is a product of both. IT organisations have always focused on core service delivery but the extent to which they embrace our concept of building brand equity will affect how they go about their business, how they assess their performance, how they maintain the balance between service and brand and how they are perceived by the business. Together these form the service engine.

Figure 3.1 shows the ten-point framework for assessing this service engine and for assessing IT service providers of all kinds. Consider the framework as a mechanism for both gaining a more complete understanding of the total business experience and at the same time conducting a skills audit of the service provider. As before the radar diagram shows a higher or 'ideal' level of skill which is always set at 100% and a lower rating which is the 'assessment' of performance relative to the ideal.

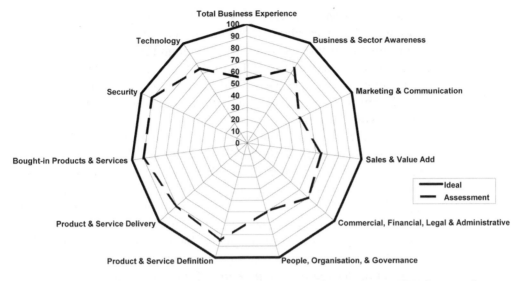

FIGURE 3.1   *An assessment of a service engine using the ITDYNAMICS™ framework*

This holistic approach provides a more complete understanding of the business experience. The assessment framework for the service engine can provide a good approximation of the total business experience and give us ideas on how the gaps in the service excellence model can be closed.

The left-hand side of the ten-point assessment framework describes the five key aspects of the core and actual IT product or service. These are as follows.

- Product and service definition: requirements, design and specification.
- Product and service delivery: systems development, systems integration, operations and service desk.
- Bought-in products and services: supplies and supplier management.
- Security: business security, IT security and business continuity.
- Technology: the technical platform.

This represents 'soup to nuts' in terms of the design and delivery of IT products and services but when the industry has talked about service excellence in the past it will typically have been addressing 'product and service definition' and 'product and service delivery' which encompass the conventional lifecycle of systems requirements definition, systems development, systems integration and IT operations. There are many methodologies and frameworks in this area and this is also predominantly the area addressed by the standards bodies. ITIL in its latest v3 service lifecycle format can now clearly be seen to be almost totally focused on product and service definition (service strategy and service design) and product and service delivery (service operation and service transition). Although ITIL v3 talks about a 'unified service model' it remains firmly an operations framework. Furthermore, although ITIL talks about providing a 360° view of service it is still very IT-focused and very much for IT practitioners in the operations field; none of us should have a problem with this provided we understand these limitations and maintain an overall business focus.

Systems (or solutions) and service design and delivery will rarely be separated in the mind of the business manager. The business manager will be aware when there is an IT related problem but they will not try to work out the cause. These are the core IT activities so we are not suggesting that these activities are in some way no longer important, just that we have to get everything right and should recognise that this area only represents two out of the ten areas that we need to assess in order to assess the business experience or to meet the business need.

If we consider the total population of methodologies and frameworks for IT management including Control Objectives for Information and Related Technologies (COBIT), eSCM, ISPL, ITIL, MSP, PRINCE2 and the SFIA framework, and map the cumulative wisdom against the assessment framework for the service engine we can see that this yields a very low total business experience rating (see Figure 3.2).

This should not surprise us because although all of the frameworks and methods mentioned above are IT-focused, there is much overlap and we already know that they do not guarantee success. The assessment framework considers services from a business rather than an IT perspective and so it is designed to meet a more comprehensive set of needs. From this we can see that if we are looking to improve on our performance we

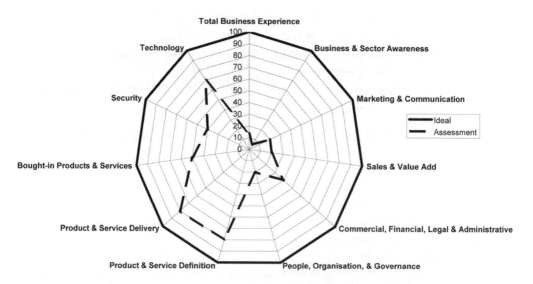

FIGURE 3.2   *The business experience implied by using the IT frameworks*

need to look at other specialist and management disciplines rather than just IT, or at least we should look at IT differently. If we consider the work of Ornstein and Sperry (see Buzan 2001), we would assume that IT people are predominantly 'left brained' with a bias toward logic, numbers, structure, analysis, lists etc. As a consequence we see that it should be no surprise that these methods are only concerned with the left-hand side of the framework and the right-hand side is largely unsupported. However the business is likely to have no such left-brain bias and will be open to the creative skills, will expect to understand the value being created and require a more holistic approach.

The right-hand side of the ten-point assessment framework describes the aspects of business experience that drive brand equity. These will be an essential part of the business expectation and included in this group are the following.

- Business and sector awareness: the extent to which the services organisation understands the business and its strategy.
- Marketing and communication: the ability to communicate with the business.
- Sales and value-add: the ability to identify investment that will add value to the business.
- Commercial, financial, legal and administrative: the financial planning and accounting, extent of compliance etc.
- People, organisation and governance: the culture, calibre and motivation of its people and the governance structure for the service delivery organisation.

If we can assess each of the ten aspects of service with some objectivity then we can profile the total business experience. If we derive an average score for the core service and an average score for the brand equity we can then calculate a value for the total business experience using the following formula:

Total business experience (%) = (Core service (%) × Brand equity (%))/100

This means that if either the core service or brand equity is assessed to be zero, then the resulting total business experience will be zero. So if you were thinking that because your core service is first class you do not need to anything further to develop brand you would be wrong. Equally a good brand will not mask a poor core service.

Try this for yourself. Although you do not yet have a complete understanding of how we make our assessment, use the blank framework (Figure 3.3) to assess the services that you may provide under each of our headings, ask others in your organisation to do the same and compare your views, then ask your business customers to give their opinion of your services. If you represent the business make an assessment of your service provider and ask one of their representatives to assess the service they provide. Each time use a fresh copy of the blank framework so that opinion is not influenced by someone else's view. Try to work out averages for core service (on the left) and brand equity (on the right), and work out a value for the total business experience.

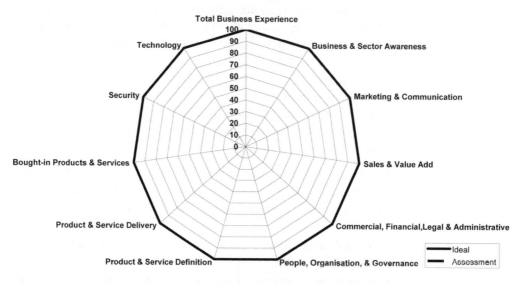

FIGURE 3.3   *A blank ITDYNAMICS™ assessment framework*

Clearly when ITDYNAMICS™ undertakes an assessment of an IT organisation the process is rigorous but this little example will probably have sufficed to expose some interesting differences in perception. Try to understand the reasons for them. Are there differences of opinion between the providers of the service and those receiving them and does this account for your current concerns? Is there a pattern in terms of the perceived strengths and weaknesses of the service provider? Is the overall assessment of the total business experience different to any customer satisfaction surveys or assessments using other methods? Do you think there would be business value in developing an improvement programme? By undertaking such an improvement programme do you think that some of the gaps in your service excellence model would be closed?

The ten-point assessment framework is essentially the same for commercial IT organisations as it is for internal IT organisations: the same skills are needed but in different quantities. Internal IT organisations do not talk about **marketing** or **sales** yet recognise the need to **communicate** and **add value**. These skills will be important to all businesses. Some corporate cultures will consider the branding of IT to be inappropriate or even offensive. However, just because a culture may find **branding** offensive, do not assume that **brand equity** is unimportant in that culture. These differences must be understood and dealt with appropriately.

The assessment process will be undertaken at a point in time and as such it will assess the methods used and compare them with what is considered to be best practice at that time. Clearly the assessment process must be updated regularly with information about best practice from the news, books and other professional journals, course material, standards bodies where appropriate, government agencies, professional bodies, trade associations, government legislation and through the experience of working with good and bad organisations worldwide.

Only by considering all of these aspects can we fully understand the strengths and weaknesses of an organisation and decide which aspects of the service to improve in order to maximise the business experience and close any gaps. Today many IT organisations are finding that whilst in benchmark comparisons their technical performance is ranked high and the results of customer satisfaction surveys are high, the anecdotal evidence from the business is less flattering. There are many examples in IT where delivery of the core service is already very high and further improvement becomes inordinately expensive. Improvements to aspects of the service that enhance brand rather than the core service can greatly improve the business experience and these changes can be relatively cost-effective. As a consequence IT organisations are looking at their services more holistically and recognising that the total business experience is more than just systems and services design and delivery.

We use the ten-point assessment framework to help us to assess the strengths and weaknesses of an IT organisation, not just from an expert perspective but also from the perspectives of a variety of internal and external stakeholders. By comparing these different views we can often establish a link between cause and effect. This is powerful because we can demonstrate the effect of actions (or a lack of them) and build a case for improvement or change. In this way we would expect to reach consensus or convergence in terms of the relative strengths and weaknesses of a service provider. We can advise on what needs to be done and the actions that represent the best business value to take forward over the plan period.

So far we have only dealt with the headings and basic principles but in the following pages we introduce more detail to guide someone who may wish to make an assessment. First an introduction to the three-stage approach of establishing the business context, undertaking the assessment and dealing with the outputs; this will have long-term significance whereas the detail will always reflect the issues, methods and technologies of the day.

ESTABLISHING THE BUSINESS CONTEXT AND PROJECT INITIATION

We must first understand the business, what it does, its size, number and type of business units and locations, what is important to the business, what the business is trying to achieve, where the business units sell their products or services, what the market is like for their products and services (including the PFEST aspects), market trends, who has what responsibility (an organisation chart is useful), major areas of cost, revenue streams and where profits are made today or will be made tomorrow. It may be necessary to develop an understanding of the business strategy including business objectives, planning mix (positioning, profitability and performance), the marketing mix (product or market segmentation, pricing, place or channel, promotion) or service mix (people, process, physical evidence, periodicity) and the competitive environment (suppler, direct rivals, substitute product or services, new entrants and buyers), together with an analysis of competitor activity.

It is good to have an understanding of the state of maturity of the business and company performance. There are various maturity models and we might choose to position the client business within the context of the most appropriate model. For example the following stages may be applicable: formation, early success, growth, maturity, decline and demise. It is necessary to examine the reasons for the state of maturity. In terms of business performance we might look at performance against plan over the last three years, forward expectation, the major drivers of revenue and growth. Take the opportunity to find out what KPIs are used to monitor day-to-day performance of the business. Establish whether there has been any material change in ownership of any part of the business and the impact that this had on maturity, performance and plans, and similarly whether there are any joint ventures or similar arrangements and the impact that these had.

Finally we need to understand the business issues from a boardroom perspective: internal, external and IT specific. Regardless of who requested the assessment (i.e. the business or the service provider) we must also fully understand the reasons for this being requested and the scope, objectives and any constraints for the work (e.g. business units, countries, functions, outputs, cost, timescales etc.).

At the conclusion of this phase we should compile a list of assumptions, opportunities and threats as part of the SWOT (strengths, weaknesses, opportunities, threats) summary to provide the context for the IT assessment and validate our understanding of the both the situation and the requirement with the business sponsor. Finally we deal with the tasks associated with project initiation and mobilisation.

AN APPROACH TO THE ASSESSMENT

We look at each aspect of service, we consider the many skills needed in an IT organisation and structure our analysis around the service excellence model and the ten-point assessment framework for the service engine. There are four perspectives that we like to capture when conducting this analysis: (i) the expert perspective (to make an independent assessment by comparing procedures with best practice); (ii) the IT perspective (from the people from the departments or organisations providing the IT services to understand their current practices and what they think works and what does not); (iii) the business perspective (from managers and users within the business units to find out what it is like to receive the service); and finally (iv) the views of suppliers and any other key external stakeholders (to find out what it is like to be a third party in the relationship with the business or between the service provider and the business).

The most effective assessments incorporate the four perspectives combining the views of carefully chosen internal and external stakeholders at all levels. The objective is to achieve a complete 360° view of the IT services in order to fully understand the strengths and weaknesses although sometimes we have to accept client-imposed constraints on who we can talk to during the assessment.

Stakeholders can be as diverse as board members, business unit managers, corporate strategy groups, business people and those involved in the delivery of supported business processes, suppliers, IT management and staff, shareholders, community groups and even conceivably politicians and central and local government departments. Their interests will be equally diverse (e.g. cost, business value, innovation, competitive edge, clarity of business requirement, product or service quality, responsiveness, clear organisational responsibilities, high-level skills, business continuity, employment opportunity, financial reward or compensation, prestige, power and influence, dividends, capital growth, market share, job satisfaction, clear contractual and financial arrangements, the environment, low unemployment etc.). It is worthwhile spending some time agreeing on the scope of the assessment and ensuring that all key stakeholders within the scope of the work have been correctly and completely identified and that their likely needs can be anticipated.

We meet with them or their representatives on a one-to-one basis (in person or on the telephone) or in focus groups. We establish their needs, experience of the current level of service and their interests, concerns and perspectives on detailed aspects of the ten-point assessment framework. We look for consistency in terms of the concerns. When different interest groups have the same concerns we know that we have found something of substance. It is usually better to disregard an isolated remark (unless supported by experienced expert opinion) as this may require the stakeholder who raised it to justify the claim on their own and it may not be of any consequence to others. We look for patterns in terms of who is saying what.

We would normally start by getting an overview of the IT organisation. The first business stakeholder to be interviewed is usually the principal business representative who is able to articulate improvement objectives. They would be followed by others in the business who will provide the most appropriate level of detail. Armed with the views of the business community we would then follow up with a more detailed look at the

IT services provider. We might also have discussions with the business' customer and supplier representatives; these are worthwhile because they sometimes lead to the identification of new business opportunities and can sometimes even provide us with useful intelligence about our competitors. Some iteration will be required as we home in on areas of opportunity.

This approach will enable us to understand not just what key stakeholders think about the services on both sides of the demand and supply equation but also the reasons for this in terms of cause and effect. Comparison with industry trends also tells us what opportunities the organisation might consider in order to improve not just stakeholder satisfaction but also business competitiveness.

THE OUTPUTS

The analysis enables all stakeholders to reach agreement on an organisation's strengths and weaknesses and a unifying action plan converging on performance improvement. The same analysis might also lead to new insights by understanding which business units are currently best served and the relative performance of key suppliers to the IT services provider.

The output from this analysis is a profiling of the IT services and a comprehensive, well-considered and universally supported performance improvement programme for IT in the business. The performance improvement programme will be based upon those initiatives that are perceived to have the greatest beneficial impact at the most affordable price.

This framework is as comprehensive, broad and deep as may be required simply because it examines the total business experience and can embrace all published methods, international standards and known best practice. It is easy to understand, is easy to communicate, is easy to use and it can easily assimilate any new thinking or insights that would benefit the industry. IT is still a young sector and one of constant flux and change as new technologies emerge. As a consequence this assessment process is particularly appropriate as it focuses not just on the 'what' and the 'how' but also looks at the net effect. What is the point of method if the outcomes do not include improvement that can be experienced by the business?

THE DETAIL OF THE ANALYSIS

The following sections deal with each of the ten areas to be assessed and the development of the action plan. At the end we list some special situations requiring different treatment. For each skill set we discuss leadership implications. We tend to consider that there is only room for one leader in an organisation but in fact we need someone to lead each of the ten areas. In some we may identify the need for more than one leading role. In smaller organisations it may be the same person for all, but the ideas may help these people to address their blind spots as all of the skills must be developed if we are to aspire to service excellence. When looking at leadership we return to the theme of 'closeness to the business' as being the single biggest factor contributing to success and consider what this means in terms of the skill set under discussion.

Business and sector awareness

At the business context and project initiation stage of the assessment assignment we took the trouble to get ourselves acquainted with the past, current and future business situation. In undertaking the assessment we establish the state of awareness of our IT service provider of the business and industry sector within which the business operates. The understanding of the wider business context also enables us to have more fruitful discussions with the business unit managers.

You may be asking what this has to do with IT service provision or for that matter with the provision of any other service. In fact it can enhance every other aspect of delivering service mentioned in this book; this applies not just to our knowledge of the primary business sector but of any others that may be relevant to the business for whatever reason at any time. Many organisations have operations or interests in multiple sectors; if the same service provider is used it is essential that it has a sound understanding of all of them.

Awareness enables us to quickly shortlist potential product suppliers that would otherwise require product research and evaluation so saving money and time. The knowledge of other sectors may be relevant where the sector is going through change and different experiences are needed, especially where the business is addressing a new market with different dynamics and different suppliers or where the business is making a major acquisition. It is quite disturbing to find people working for and being paid by a business that fail to understand anything of significance about the business or its environment. It is equally disturbing to think that organisations that recognise that their business is changing sometimes fail to bring in people who can help them to move up the learning curve quickly. Knowledge of the economy, the primary market and ancillary markets, and knowledge of the progress of the business itself can generate ideas and strategies that can move a business from being ordinary to being a leader.

Knowledge of the macro-environment

We first need to establish how the business and the service provider relate to the macro-environment (i.e. from the market and the PFEST perspectives). This has more to do with the trading environment than with the business itself. Whilst there is always a national context this must be set within the global picture and this can become quite complex. We must understand how we must operate as a business or service provider as well as how we position ourselves in the global context in today's market conditions.

Knowledge of the meso-environment

Here we are concerned with the industry in particular: the value chain, the competition, the nature of the market and the competitive environment. An awareness of the business and the business sector provides a context for the work we do, it enables us to focus on particular areas, make day-to-day tactical decisions and judge the long-term relevance. Through business and sector awareness we are able to understand the intricacies of how markets compare, how a market operates and where the value is added. Perhaps it allows us to decide when it is safe to make a decision on our own to save time and when we need to consult with others.

Knowledge of the micro-environment

Here we are concerned with the business itself. We should be aware of: material changes of ownership, joint ventures or similar arrangements, the company structure, the needs of the key business stakeholders for the services being provided; the competitive environment; the business strategy, the stage in the development of the business; recent company performance, major change programmes and their significance, the financial situation (income, profits over the period, major drivers of revenue and profit growth) and future forecasts of performance; product or service range, performance by product or service and market, segment or geography (product and market segmentation); main business processes, corporate KPIs used to monitor the performance of the business; and assumptions, opportunities and threats. If the business is moving into new sectors then it must understand the drivers and major goals and work with service providers who are familiar with the new sector and who can help the business to rapidly meet these new needs.

This aspect of the assessment is to understand the business need and to determine the extent to which the services provider understands the business and the business sector. A lack of knowledge can lead to incorrect judgments being made: knowledge of the business really, and frequently, does make a difference.

There is always an assumption that internal services providers have the advantage over external service providers. In fact internal service providers can often be less knowledgeable than a well-briefed external service provider. Equally there are external service providers who have never been briefed on the client or client business and who have not bothered to undertake any kind of research of their own. A well-informed and business-aware service provider will always be seen to be a more relevant and more valuable resource than one that is not.

Most of the large service providers segment their business by industry sector so for example they may have a division focusing on the financial services sector, and another on the retail sector etc. This can be a way of accumulating and developing industry-specific knowledge. Other organisations may specialise in one sector only while others will restrict themselves to employing only seasoned practitioners with experience of many sectors. When selecting suppliers we have to ask whether we are looking to learn from others in the same sector, introduce ideas from another industry or maybe introduce new ideas or new disciplines not previously tried in order to create new improvement opportunities.

The critical information set for the business and the sector

The business environment and all industry sectors are information rich. Each business is dependant upon information of some kind. Back in the 1980s the business schools at Harvard and the Massachusetts Institute of Technology (Sloane Business School) were leaders in the field of the thinking that leads to defining the information that supports a business. The general view in those days was one of a business vision driving objectives and critical success factors.

Back in 1985 the author was employed by British Rail to first realign the IT to better support their business sectors and then to advise the board on IT investment. A few high-profile professors are often useful for getting the attention of a board of directors so a couple of MIT people were invited to make a presentation. British Rail had spent a lot of money over a number of years trying to realign systems with no success. The systems only supported the information needs of the functions of the organisation that in most cases had specified and developed the solutions and some of the management information was sustaining several old organisational regimes. The author had undertaken a similar assignment previously at Whitbread which also had needed to realign its IT solutions to address a major restructuring of its business and the way to do this is to work both conceptually in terms of general frameworks and at a detailed level to engage with the business on a level that makes sense in terms of how they wish to run their business. The author knew that at the time MIT would talk about the work they had done on vision, objectives and critical success factors, the author had used this successfully at Whitbread but had to take it to the next level. Where MIT talked about critical success factors, the author talked about defining and supporting a critical information set. Whereas critical success factors made sense strategically, the critical information set made sense in real terms at the next level down. This would enable us to look at the information systems and databases that would feed really useful information to the businesses. The usefulness of the approach was recognised immediately and management systems were soon in place for all business sectors together with some new ideas on ticketing and ticket pricing, passenger information systems, train operations systems, track and infrastructure management systems etc.

The railway business embraced many diverse activities and the business structure was complex. Typical analytical approaches lead to great confusion as had been the case at British Rail before the author became involved. Defining the critical information set is a straightforward way of tackling the complexity and the author has since used the idea on many occasions with large and small organisations alike. The way this is done is described in the following.

At the top we still have vision, business objectives and critical success factors but only in the smallest businesses is it that simple. Critical success factors can be numerous and varied. On the one hand managers make assumptions about the business environment and they need to have information that substantiates these assumptions or provide the necessary information to advise the business that there may be a need to modify an assumption. For example a business may make assumptions about the cost of labour, the cost of raw materials, the major industry suppliers and sources of material, the economics surrounding the competitive environment and the price and profit per mile and assumptions about the cost of borrowing or interest rates. As this was a publicly owned business, there was also a need to have a view on the propensity of the government of the day to invest in rail transportation. We call this the critical assumption set. Macro-, meso- and micro-information would need to be gathered and reported to be able to advise management on these factors.

Next there are the decisions that management need to make over the budget period and the information that is required to support these decisions. Perhaps there would be a need to upgrade the maintenance of a line or route in order to increase standards of service. Perhaps new infrastructure is required (e.g. a new station, a new car park, a new freight terminal, new track or new rolling stock). These require mainly micro-information but it would draw heavily upon the critical assumption set. We called this the critical decision set.

At any one time a large business will have a number of change programmes that are live. Supporting the management of each of these, or all of these, there will be a programme office that is monitoring and reporting progress. This is referred to in this context as the critical business change set.

The transactional data that reflects the current volume of business being processed in terms of purchases, sales, cash flow, profitability etc. we call the critical business activity data set.

Finally there are the metrics relating to business performance based upon efficiency data and benchmark comparisons (e.g. punctuality statistics, train cancellations, signals passed at danger etc.). This is referred to as the critical business performance set.

Together these form the critical information set as illustrated in Figure 3.4.

Today, most organisations manage using some kind of business dashboard. The board of the business will have regular feeds of

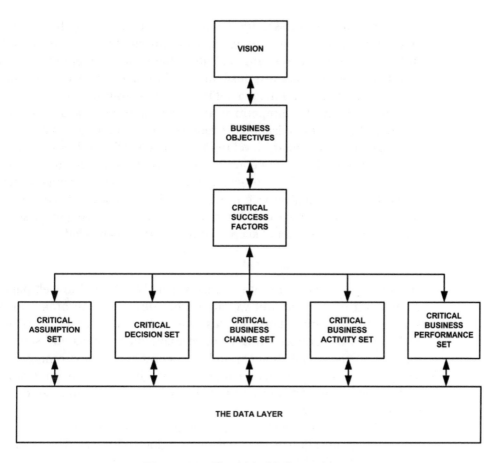

FIGURE 3.4   *The critical information set*

information on external market data as well as headline data on the progress of the business. This is where the critical information set is reported drawing heavily on the 'data layer' (see the section on marketing and communications). Our discussions with the business and IT service provider will enable us to understand how well the critical information set is defined and used.

Leadership of business and sector awareness

'Closeness to the business' is achieved by a having a common understanding of the how the business operates and the context in which the business operates. Service providers that have an understanding of the critical information set however will have a detailed understanding of how they can support the business. They might also have their own critical information set which will enable them to monitor their own service to the business.

There are two complementary leadership roles. The first may be within the IT services provider's organisation encouraging relevance (understanding business critical data), awareness (the global market, industry context and own performance) and agility (ability to identify and respond quickly to changes). Within the business there might be a leadership role to take responsibility for briefing the service provider about the company and the market in which it operates. This may extend to issues relating to competitive advantage and so a degree of trust between the two organisations is required. This latter role may be the responsibility of the board-level representative for IT services or it could be the responsibility of someone in the corporate communications area. Regular business briefings to key members of the IT services organisation would be ideal. Small service providers with a less strategic role in the context of the business would often brief themselves on the business but the service provider should keep subcontractors fully briefed.

Marketing and communications

For non-commercial enterprises, this is usually confined to web pages, demos and newsletters but we should be thinking more broadly. Our service provider must know its business stakeholders and understand their needs; our service provider must make its products and services relevant to these stakeholders and in a competitive environment the service provider must ensure that what it offers will be understood and viewed more favourably than the offerings from other potential suppliers.

Stakeholder groups will in some way be dependent upon the service provider's organisation (e.g. for a service, product or project). The potential stakeholders will vary by business and service provider. Each group of stakeholders will have different needs depending on the stage in the life-cycle of the engagement creating many reasons to communicate. Figure 1.6 illustrated how we might express an assessment of the quality of the communication between an IT services provider and various parts of the business, its customers, suppliers and groups within its own organisation and the extent to which it falls short of what is expected or what would be ideal. Figure 3.5 is a similar example of an assessment for a different type of service provider again illustrating the quality of the communication with its key stakeholders. In this example there are stakeholders who may need information about the service but the role of the service provider may be to supply the information via an intermediary (e.g. via the media, via the board or at a shareholder's meeting).

In all of these cases it becomes easy to point to potential issues that may arise in the future with stakeholders of various kinds or indeed explain how a current problem may have arisen. It is clearly important to have a good dialogue with all key stakeholders. As in all things business-focused, we should recognise that businesses change and that we must keep the stakeholder groups under review to pick up emerging key players and focus less on those that cease to be key.

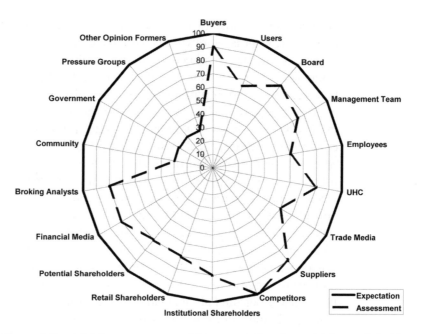

FIGURE 3.5 *A further assessment of the communications with key stakeholders*

If we communicate effectively we will understand the business requirements of our customers, the areas where we can add the most value and the areas where the most competitive advantage can be gained. In order to communicate effectively we as the service provider need to know where we are right now in terms of the market segments we support, our performance in terms of market share, our IT product and services portfolio, where our products and services sit in terms of the Boston matrix, the maturity of our products and services and where we are in terms of buyer interest and buyer attitude. We must think of communication as a two-way process: the services provider will need to ask whether it knows enough about the needs of the stakeholders and whether the stakeholders know enough about the capabilities of the services provider. If the services provider does not find out what the business wants it can never provide it. If the services provider does not tell the business enough about its products and services and what they can do for the business, the business will have to come to its own conclusions. Ries and Trout (1999) suggested that the most powerful concept in marketing is to own a word or phrase in the prospect's mind, such as BA (the world's favourite airline), Coca-Cola (the real thing), BMW (the ultimate driving machine), Nike (just do it) or even ITDYNAMICS™ (revitalising software and services organisations). In marketing jargon this is known as 'share of the mind'. Whilst you are thinking about what words you want to own, just remember that it will not work if it is perceived to be unreasonable and cannot be sustained over the longer term. The long-term aspect of this always creates the greatest difficulty as markets are in constant flux. Even success brings its own problems, for example Hoover is synonymous with a vacuum cleaner, even when it is a Dyson. Positioning can become quite complex; we are talking here about single ideas of motivation and if we were a marketing agency we would be researching the importance of our shortlisted words to the particular interest groups or stakeholder groups in the hope that they were relevant motivators, did not inadvertently exclude any key groups and did not contain any unintended 'double meanings' in any language in any country where the words would be used. This is the 'easy peasy' world of consumer marketing where most of the marketing gurus made their reputations but when marketing services the task is more complex. Do not run away with any idea of simply applying consumer-style marketing to professional services. The techniques of consumer marketing were developed in the 1960s and 1970s and were applied to cigarettes, chocolate bars and fizzy drinks. Since those heady days marketing has been successfully applied to industrial endeavours, 'not for profit' organisations and services. Smith (2005) describes the failure of simplistic approaches to strategic marketing planning in the context of complex services. Whilst he does not specifically use IT services as a complex example he suggests that complex and turbulent markets require the right combination of visionary and rational planning whilst simple stable markets respond best to incremental planning.

Relationship marketing is one of the recent labels to be applied to developing the techniques to retain or extend a profitable services business. Interestingly, even the ardent devotees of relationship marketing promote the need to consider what the service customer buys and how the service product must be designed: the core capability, the augmentation we build into it and the potential of the product. Sometimes capability is not enough. Moore (1991) described a revised technology adoption lifecycle and its validity was immediately recognised by the technology industry. He describes a product lifecycle with a gap (or 'chasm') that has to be crossed in order to reach the main market. We all know from our own experiences that our purchasing criteria will differ depending upon what we are buying. IT products are not like consumer products. Consumer product lifecycles follow the traditional pattern of early stage, growth, maturity and decline. Marketers can incrementally extend the life of a product in various ways. Moore argues that there are different dynamics in the case of technology products in the business-to-business environment. He distinguishes between the early market and the mainstream market. He argues that products move from an early adopter stage where the interest is first from technical enthusiasts who have a specialist interest and then the visionaries, to the general market where the early adopters are first the pragmatists and then the conservative (main) market. Depending on the scale of the solution, as the product moves through the phases and crosses the chasm from specialist interest to general interest it requires endorsement or it has to gain appropriate market recognition. Clearly both the traditional lifecycle model and the 'chasm model' are working together and we have to understand where we are placed relative to these two sets of dynamics at any given moment to blend the right mix of vision, incremental and rational planning.

Like all other organisations our IT services provider will have products, services and markets. It should be deploying market research techniques to understand the market requirements. If it is focused on an internal market it will be deploying business analysts. If it is a commercial organisation it will be utilising market research analysts but often as an alternative it will try to attract potential new employees with a current knowledge of the target market and key contacts. Whatever we are we summarise where we are, where we want to be and how we will get there (strategy). Where we are and where we want to be might be expressed in terms of market share or market position. Product or market segmentation can be a useful discipline. The Ansoff matrix helps us to distinguish between market penetration, market development, product development and diversification goals. We must understand where our products are in terms of their lifecycle, market acceptance and the competition. We must decide what our product strategy is and what product mix we are going to deploy. We will have a new product development (NPD) budget to back up our preferred product strategy. Our products will all have value propositions. We will have a channel or distribution plan; perhaps we will have user or affinity groups.

We may have a well-developed concept of brand. This was once characterised by a logo and an advertising budget. Gad (2001) talks about the brand mind space needing to address functional, mental, spiritual and social dimensions. He describes how we might develop a brand code covering the product benefit, the positioning, styling, mission, vision and values of the brand. Perhaps the brand extends into capability and reputation. This is much closer to business-focused IT where we advocate an holistic approach to the breadth of what might be considered to build brand equity for professional services organisations. Maybe we are at the point where we have a brand strategy and this is backed up by investment for product development, advertising and promotion. Perhaps there is a pricing strategy to back up the marketing and product strategy. The pricing strategy will influence the behaviour of the market and even fund the product investment program; a poor pricing strategy will affect the viability of the product and the business. The pricing of a service can be enormously difficult as it will depend as much on the competition as on real costs and value to the business. For a business trying to understand and compare one service with another from a different supplier can be time-consuming and inconclusive. The less we understand the service the more likely that purchase will be based on price but ironically in high-risk situations customers are much more likely to look to price as an indicator of quality (Kotler et al. 2002).

At some point the service provider will recognise the need to collaborate with others to enhance their reputation or to deliver a more comprehensive service and will have an alliances program.

There may be a marketing campaign or a communications program. Marketing mix refers to the methods used to communicate positioning, value propositions, direct the market to key channels, enhance brand, communicate pricing and address specific stakeholder needs. The more methods we use the greater our chances of successfully influencing our target market will be. Marketers think in terms of the message and the means of communication and they know that there are many reasons why a message may not arrive. They know that messages are communicated more effectively when a number of methods are deployed in an integrated way; it would be naive to assume that only one communication method was necessary to get our message across. We can choose from face to face, websites, downloads, PR using local, national or trade media, video, events (trade exhibitions, professional and business networks, road shows, breakfast, lunch or dinner meetings, entertainment, user groups, focus groups etc.), sponsorship (cause related, local interest, national interest), newsletters, brochures etc. Sherrington (2003) commits this to a formula (this really is a meeting of right and left brain) suggesting that impact leading to action (I) is a function of the number of times (n) you hear the same message (m) from different people or in different places (p), over a period of time (t), which he expresses as $I = f(n \times m \times p)t$. This has a multiplier effect (i.e. it creates a 'tipping point'). Sherrington also talks about brand vitality as being the product of brand equity and momentum and recognises the importance of brands remaining relevant as opposed to trading on their reputations. The number of times the message can be heard becomes immense when we embrace so-called connected marketing, the collective term for viral, word of mouth and buzz marketing which today can be generated from lists and are only a click away.

Whatever methods are deployed it is a good idea to manage the communication on a campaign basis: decide what you are trying to address, set some baseline measures and objectives, run the campaign and measure the result. When planning this do not forget to consider any alliances and the possible involvement of partner organisations. Traditional campaigns might be classed as a form of interruption marketing. Campaigns that rapidly evolve over time are sometimes referred to as 'episodic' campaigns. These should be constructed so as to tick the boxes in terms of maximising the impact of the campaign by using multiple media types and at the same time maximising the word of mouth element. This has been used extensively in car advertising.

Godin (2002) refers to conventional advertising as 'interruption marketing' because advertisers interrupt people who do not want to be talked to. Godin extols the value of episodic and viral marketing, coining the term 'ideavirus' for digitally augmented word of mouth. Just as we have said that we need to develop an integrated communications strategy with a multiplier effect, Godin uses the ideavirus to amplify the message. He uses this approach to tackle the 'chasm' to address the needs of the main market on the right of Moore's curve who are conservatively looking for something that works. He talks about finding and dominating a 'hive' and then developing a message that people called 'sneezers' will transmit. Traditional marketers would tell us that you dominate the market and articulate the message that we wish 'product advocates' to spread. The difference is just in the language and the fact that we are talking here about utilising digital mechanisms to help advocates spread the word. Kirby and Marsden (2006) suggest inviting opinion leaders to participate in seeding trials or market research to transform them into word of mouth advocates in order to accelerate sales. The reach of word of mouth can again be extended by the digital mechanisms associated with buzz and viral marketing.

We must understand the communications model; in other words what happens when we send a message to a target audience. There is an implicit encoding and decoding process either side of the transmission mechanism. It is easy for a message to be misconstrued by the recipient. 'Noise' can interfere with the transmission and some form of feedback should be provided so that we can be sure that the message has been received and is understood. This is the opportunity that Godin addresses with his ideavirus.

Large commercial IT service providers will have a sizeable department managing everything to do with marketing from strategy to the marketing campaigns. Even the smallest internal IT organisation should recognise the need for this discipline and the benefits it brings, not just to the supply organisation but also to the client business itself. This being the case it should be properly managed with appropriate leadership, resources, accountabilities, budget, training plan, suppliers, measurement and review. Often though the communication is unintended: Davidson (2002) tells us that communication always occurs but often it is not deliberate. He suggests that as well as advertising we communicate by our actions, behaviour, face to face, signals, products and services, word of mouth, word of web (i.e. the content of our emails, intranets and websites) and comments by other organisations. This means that we all have it within our ability to either enhance the marketing message or completely annul the message depending upon how consciously we communicate on a day-to-day basis. All of these things will influence what people think about us or what the business thinks about the IT services provider. This is the service provider's brand equity.

An IT organisation has to do more than promote itself in order to develop strong brand equity. A clear proposition from an IT service provider will be based on an analysis of needs that requires a lot of listening; think of it as a market research project. What does the business want from us? Looking at it from the business perspective we have to ask if our service provider takes the time to understand the business so that it can come up with meaningful propositions or does it simply try to push what it has? If we wanted to take the time out to understand business requirements better how would we achieve it? We could embark on a major piece of work using one of the extensive methodologies from the 1970s and 1980s but it would take a long time and would be quite expensive. The fact is that most businesses are no longer prepared to make this investment. The conventional alternative is to focus on something of value to the business and come up with a proposal that the business can consider; some major reengineering projects start from this position of selecting the solution before working out what the problem might be. We have also seen fads drive change, simply because a business has been unable or unprepared to define its needs. There is a third way.

Business analysis techniques almost always focus initially on understanding the business environment and the business strategy but then delve straight into process modelling of some kind usually using low level techniques designed for requirements planning. It is not surprising then that these techniques are typically geared toward a project, a subset of business processes, a business issue, or a known solution. Mostly business analysis in the sense of understanding what a business does and how that is supported is rarely applied to a whole business but this is exactly what is needed if we are to provide a business context for investment decisions, whether or not IT is included (and it nearly always must be included). What usually prevents us from doing this is that we have no techniques for doing it quickly. Business analysis methods get too detailed too soon. Porter's (1985) value chain gives us an overview of processes within a business but assumes too much in terms of structure, has no business points of reference and has no room for the major components of IT that drive the business. There is no justification at this early stage to invest a lot of time mapping out the whole business in detail using business analysis methods from the IT arena. What we need is a quick, business-focused way of developing that context and gaining insight into opportunities for business improvement that demonstrates business awareness and relevance potentially across the whole ecosystem and that allows limited decision making prior to perhaps embarking upon detailed business area analysis (which may not even be necessary).

Building a contextual view

IT strategy is rarely a business priority, even though it is the means by which an organisation can better understand where it needs to invest. In truth the IT strategy is nearly always the wrong starting point. The desire for an IT strategy usually comes instead from the IT professionals in an organisation; it becomes a means of building an investment case. From a business perspective the process is over-complicated to such an extent that the business sees little value in the process and is often unable to recognise the output as one that either represents their needs or their priorities.

What is needed is a business-focused approach that differs from the conventional approaches by being:

- relevant to the business;
- quick to develop;
- easy to communicate.

The ITDYNAMICS™ strategy framework

If we consider the modern context for IT, there is no complexity here. IT is simply at the centre of the business supporting its every aspect. The IT strategy framework retains this simplicity but incorporates the primary business processes and major IT components. The outer parts of the diagram contain the major process groups each of which is focused on a key stakeholder group. The IT infrastructure is represented by an inner box within which we can show applications, information or services.

This IT strategy framework contains enough detail to be able to talk about the major investments and opportunity areas at a level which will engage most board-level audiences. Although not detailed in itself it will be accurate. More detailed work will have been undertaken and abstracted and summarised at this level so that it becomes more relevant to the business audience. Without the clutter and incomprehensible 'techno-babble', all we have to do is use the important architectural and business components in the diagram to highlight the IT opportunities. Figure 3.6 shows how the starting point might look.

It is a summary chart that provides us with a reference point for our detailed business analysis and our proposed IT solutions so that we can be sure that we do not lose sight of our overall objectives. It can be used for top-down analysis and later as an abstraction of all of the key features of the business and supporting IT. It is the missing or improved level-zero model that provides the business context for case diagrams and more detailed process models. We have to acknowledge the work of various people. The framework is derived from some of the characteristics of Porter's (1985) value chain, a balanced scorecard similar to the original work of Kaplan and Norton (1996, 2004, 2006) and structured around the four most important stakeholder groups ensures that there is a balance to the IT support and the more recent ebusiness architectures pioneered by Kalakota and Robinson (1999) in the USA. It combines the objectivity of all of them but is still confined within a usefully small diagram. The four stakeholder groups most commonly used are those in the illustration: customers, investors, suppliers and people. This can vary, especially in 'not for profit' and heavily regulated industries. The framework can be used to record primary business processes in a manner that is consistent with our context diagram, to describe the fundamental features of the proposed IT infrastructure, to show the core applications or services that will be used to support the business and to show the key information areas (not illustrated).

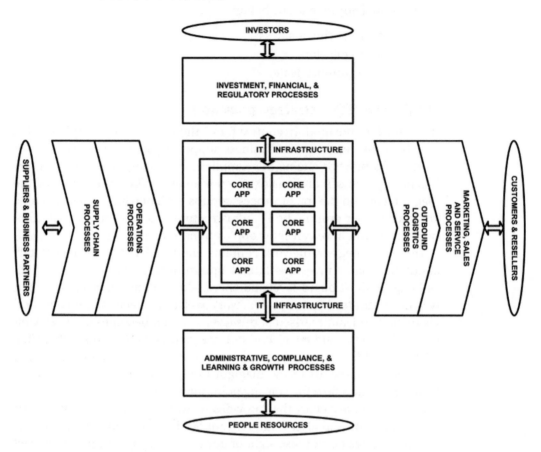

FIGURE 3.6   *The ITDYNAMICS™ IT strategy framework*

We can start by defining the processes that 'face' our key stakeholder groups. Typically organisations (of whatever size) have great difficulty agreeing what the core processes are. Often we become constrained in our thinking about process by the current organisational structure and the existing departmental domains which can become fiefdoms that defend old working practices. The stakeholders we are looking for on the other hand will demand simplicity and clear delivery objectives allowing the business to decide how this might be achieved and what organisation might be appropriate. Having a framework unconstrained by the current organisation provides a useful starting point to think about the business more simply. The customer-facing processes will include key sales, marketing and service processes. These may be backed up by any outbound logistics processes (e.g. warehousing and distribution). The supplier-facing processes will define supply chain and supporting operations activities.

The investor-facing activities will describe the financial and regulatory processes. Finally, people processes include organisational administration, process compliance and learning and growth processes associated with training and education. These high-level or level-one processes are inserted into the strategy framework illustration in the appropriate box between the IT infrastructure and the stakeholder groups. For example in the box containing the words 'OPERATIONS PROCESSES' on the left-hand side of the illustration, we would insert the names of the five to ten key business processes in the operations area of the business. Having agreed what the core processes are, we can consider the extent to which each is currently supported by technology, should be supported in the future and how the infrastructure is to be specified. We can use the diagram to search for the important end-to-end processes that are capable of streamlining the organisation, search for the opportunities for disintermediation perhaps by closer integration with a supplier or customer and ensure that resource utilisation and financial implications throughout the business are accurately recorded. Just as we can connect or join value chains we can dismember and join IT strategy frameworks to create extended enterprises. As we connect the enterprise frameworks together they take on the appearance of complex molecules. Thus we can view the business from different perspectives and ensure that solutions cover the whole of the ecosystem.

An example from the 'not for profit' sector is illustrated in Figure 3.7. Here inbound and outbound logistics are less significant and have been replaced by other processes relating to their key stakeholders of international board, membership, general council and treasury. Note that the actual processes have been changed to protect the identity of the client organisation.

The value of this framework is its ability to communicate and engage with the business and to ensure a balanced understanding of the key activities of the enterprise. This 'not for profit' example was used to better understand the total business requirement for solutions. Later it was used to illustrate the impact that an accurate and up-to-date membership database would have on the UK operation. There were going to be political difficulties surrounding the adoption and implementation of a membership database and the concept was going to be a hard sell to the general council. The diagram was used to illustrate the number of processes that would become easier once a database was in place. The members of the general council all had their particular interests and in this way it could be demonstrated that the database would be for the universal good of the organisation. This 'redlining' of the strategy framework diagram can be used to identify all manner of changes and impact without extraneous detail although it is helpful to ensure that there is a sufficient understanding in the mind of the person presenting the model to be able to talk convincingly about the benefits. An example of 'redlining' is illustrated in Figure 3.8.

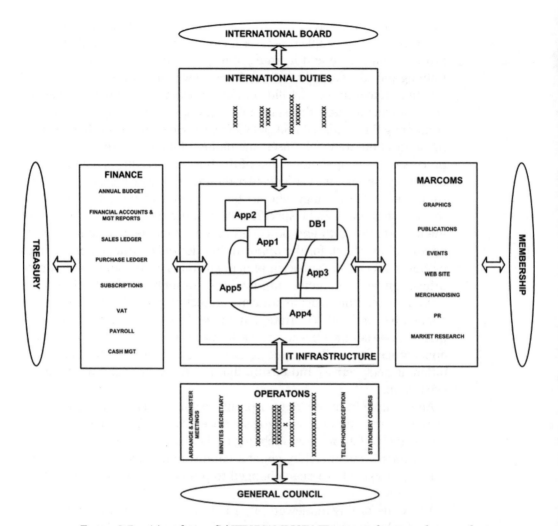

FIGURE 3.7 *A 'not for profit' ITDYNAMICS™ IT strategy framework example*

At the next level of detail below this strategy framework analysts will use the most appropriate methods to model and specify the detail of the processes and applications solutions or services. These methods will probably include case diagrams, business activity modelling and decomposition methods. The Unified Modeling Language (UML) may be used for this purpose. However complex the work of analysing and specifying the requirement, the ITDYNAMICS™ strategy framework will always provide the business context for both business and IT components and thus enable the wood to be separated from the trees. Decomposition and abstraction help to redefine key business processes and define a business context for the core IT components of IT infrastructure, applications or services and data. Most importantly it also provides a vehicle for discussing the important activities of the business and its efficiency and effectiveness thus establishing the means of creating insight and opportunity.

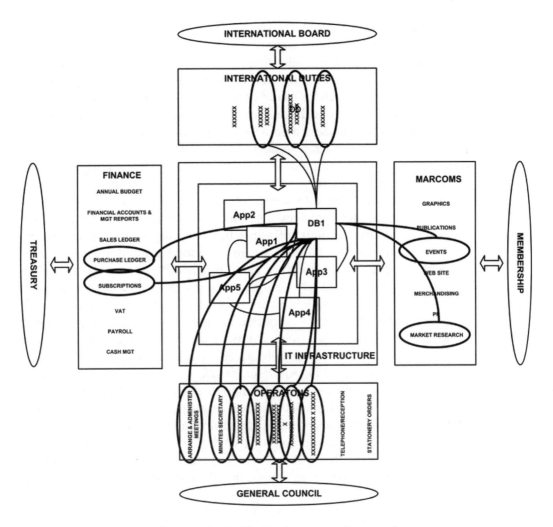

FIGURE 3.8   *Redlining the strategy framework*

Mostly businesses are no longer concerned with systems development planning but with the identification, integration and deployment of potential solutions. It is generally acknowledged that there are advantages in minimising the number of applications systems (or solutions) used by a business. Fewer solutions mean fewer interfaces and a simplified integration task. Larger businesses can have many hundreds of applications largely because of the legacy of previous implementations, company acquisitions, old products that may have to be maintained etc. Most businesses would recognise that the applications architecture is costing them money in terms of maintenance and support costs or lost opportunity (lack of agility). These organisations would readily accept that there is a concept of core applications that is worth defining and representing in a way that enables it to be raised and discussed, perhaps in an abstracted (summary) form, at senior levels.

A service-oriented architecture will need to be approached in a similar way by always looking to simplify the IT construct or ontology to ensure that the IT implications follow logically from the business context. In this case there should be strong links from the decomposition of process to the services being orchestrated and the level-one process structure is a sensible abstraction of the services. The inner area will identify the key services and the linkages across the ecosystem of businesses.

Clearly in these cases, whether such linkages are long-term or transitory, a compatible or common IT infrastructure can be important. In the strategy framework the inner area of core applications or services is surrounded by a layer to separately identify the IT infrastructure. This infrastructure layer provides the vehicle for talking about the hardware and telecommunications infrastructure, the operating system software, information security features, the presentation layer and the pervasive or common utility applications required by the business or ecosystem. The scope of each model will be up for discussion, for example does each business unit operate within its own legacy infrastructure or does it get absorbed into some corporate architecture? Are we considering a single business or an extended enterprise of permanent or transitory businesses? Technology is considered in a later chapter but here we can note the high-level requirements. We may be looking to provide a state-of-the-art architecture, a distributed architecture based on 'standard' technology and commercial packages or we may be looking to minimise our dependence on a mature architecture of bespoke applications.

Government regulation and international requirements for compliance are increasing and these can be accommodated in the framework by ensuring that relevant processes are visible. We are thus able to consider the means by which we embed or underpin processes (and relevant government legislation) to create a suitably compliant or controlled environment.

In summary then we start with a vision and strategy, define the principal external stakeholders, translate this strategy into operational (functional) terms by defining key processes, define the key features of the IT infrastructure, identify the principle components of the applications or services architecture and add the data model or the information ontology. Without extraneous detail we can define a whole business or, by linking the strategy frameworks of different businesses, define extended enterprises. Left to its own devices the business will be in a constant state of flux responding to changes to the business environment in which it operates as well as changes to processes. Sometimes planned but often responding to need dynamically as people try to satisfy new and emerging requirements, the resulting IT architecture in its entirety is perhaps an example of a 'complex adaptive system' (the term used by Beinhocker (2007)) that is ever changing to support the changing needs of the business. The IT strategy framework is thus an ideal model to use regularly in conjunction with business managers to capture and to understand what is happening and to allow the business and the IT services provider to intervene in order to introduce improvement.

We use this straightforward framework to represent the whole business and to stimulate the all-important dialogues with business management. It will be underpinned by more detail in terms of processes and data but the simple diagram enables us to deal with complex businesses in a straight-forward and timely manner. We can rapidly develop an outline IT strategy or carry out a sanity check on an existing IT strategy. We might stray into specific areas in order to explore specific problems or opportunities in more detail but the recommendations will be expressed in the context of the business ecosystem and with relevance to the business strategy. Not forgetting the context diagram, we must also be prepared to challenge and improve this business strategy and if necessary help to deliver business benefits. As in any complex adaptive system any gap will be filled. If gaps are not anticipated and filled in a planned way they will be addressed by tactical solutions which in the long term may become problematic.

In the past business schools have used a triangle to distinguish between the different process classes in an organisation (i.e. strategy and planning, management and operational-level processes). Later we recognised the importance of technology in delivering process and the author represented this idea in the form of Miller's triangle (see Figure 3.9). Rather like the context diagram and the IT strategy framework, Miller's triangle is also the basis of much automation and of improvement to many real and virtual businesses. Expressed in words, we can say that 'technology delivers knowledge (by application systems or services) to support processes undertaken by people as directed by the business'.

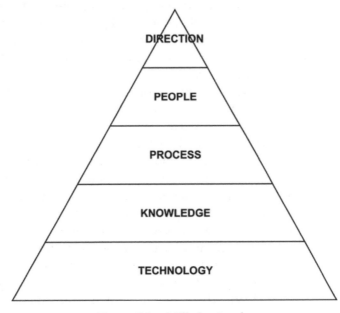

FIGURE 3.9 *Miller's triangle*

The author recently discovered that this was remarkably similar to the '4P model' as described by Liker (2004). This is a four-layer model which has problem solving at the apex, people and partners below that, then process, and finally philosophy on the base layer. Although developed independently and for different purposes, there is a striking similarity in the logic being used by both models.

Business process management is a partial implementation of Miller's triangle. The architecture typically has four layers. The presentation layer is supplied by the IT infrastructure component of our IT strategy framework, the business processes by the outer parts of the framework and the knowledge by the application systems or services defined within the inner core. The lowest level is the data layer; at this level it is important that we use techniques that bring clarity rather than those that introduce unnecessary complexity. Process analysis techniques have been adapted to be used at a high level and can work well. Data has always been more problematic so it is worth explaining how we have adapted data analysis techniques to bring additional clarity at the strategic level.

The strategic data layer

The data layer was a critical component of any IT architecture in the 1970s and 1980s when we had unsophisticated and labour-intensive database management systems. The disciplines largely fell into disuse with the advent of relational databases, enterprise resource management systems and SQL. With the need to harness and manage not just data but **knowledge** we now need to look once more at how we can bring structure and completeness to this whole area. Today it is sometimes referred to as an ontology defining individuals (instances of objects), classes (sets or collections of objects), attributes (properties or characteristics attributable to objects) and relationships (between objects). This area again is developing rapidly especially in the document management area.

If we are to avoid the silo effect within the application area we must consider the data layer when developing strategy, but rather than micromanaging as we used to, we now macro-manage. By so doing we can ensure that the full scope of the requirement is being addressed, data is defined once, can be shared and is assigned to a core application or service for management. To achieve this we need first to understand the nature of the data within the business and structure it by identifying major entities and information areas based on clusters of related entities. This speeds up the analysis and simplifies the integration of core applications and data interfaces, any knowledge management and the critical information set (and management reporting) requirements. The technique that can be used for this is the 'clustered entity model' according to Feldman and Miller (1986). There continues be a requirement to think about or even manage data in this way.

Consider an entity model for a discrete area of a manufacturing business as shown in Figure 3.10. The scope of this model only represents orders, contracts and installations; consider then how complex the model that represents the whole of the business could be.

Clustered entity modelling helps us to overcome this complexity. We can simplify the partial model by applying the rules of abstraction to reduce this to two entities (known as major entities) and a single information area entity as shown in Figure 3.11. The technique involves observing the relationships between entities, identifying logical clusters and abstracting these to create a set we call an information area that maintains the same logical relationships to the major entities. Major entities tend to be identifiable by observing one-to-many relationships away from the entity in question, in this case away from the 'CUSTOMER' and 'PRODUCT OR SERVICE' entities.

So if we need to build the bigger picture in order to understand the data implications or ontology of a whole business, we should be content with something that is complete, in that it will include all known major entities and information areas, but not necessarily detailed (see Figure 3.12).

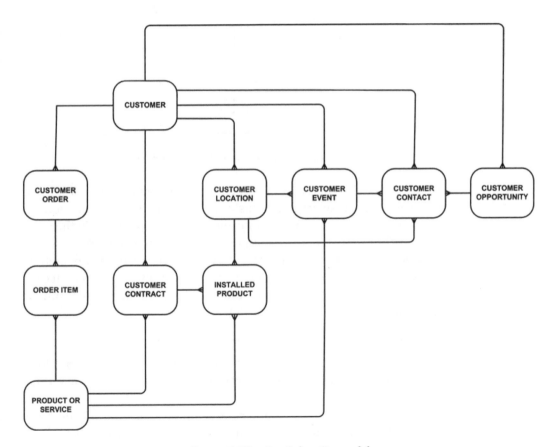

FIGURE 3.10 *Partial entity model*

The clustered entity model allows us to work on a broad canvas without the distraction of unnecessary detail thus helping us to define scope and maintain clarity. The technique can be used bottom-up by identifying desired entities and clustering and abstracting as demonstrated or with practice by an experienced analyst it can be used top-down to suggest the required detail. Rarely at this level would we define attributes but a skilled analyst will be aware of the relationship implications that attributes will have and the impact on the formation of the clusters or information areas.

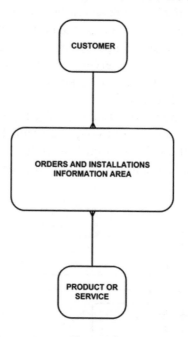

FIGURE 3.11 *Clustered partial model*

This technique has helped to restructure some major companies. It has also enabled us to select many business solutions by mapping required information areas to supported information areas. Incidentally the same clustering and abstraction techniques can be applied to process and services. The models illustrated above use the entity relationship notation because it is easier to show the 'one-to-many' relationships and hence the clustering technique but abstracted data and process can both be represented within the UML notation.

Leadership in marketing and communication

Ries and Trout (1993) suggested that marketing is not a battle of products but a battle of perceptions. If we want to change the way people think about us this requires effort.

As can be seen from this chapter the required skills not only embrace traditional marketing techniques but also extend into high-end business analysis methods. Leadership then is sought in both areas.

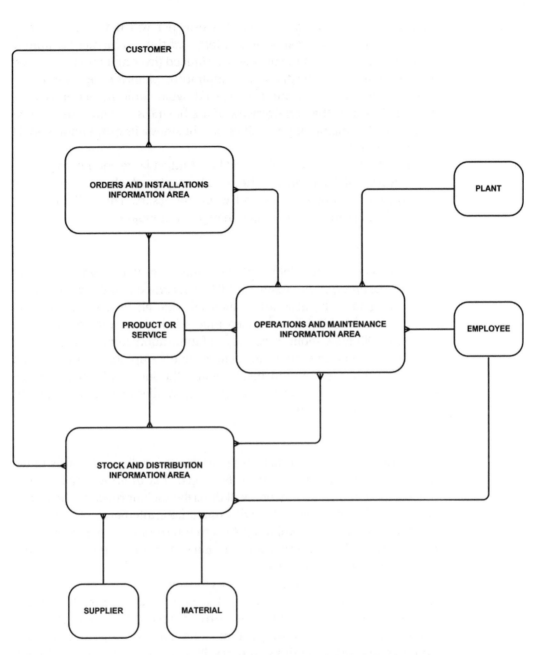

FIGURE 3.12   *Clustered entity model of a whole business*

The marketing leadership will ensure that the service is perceived to be relevant to the business and that the business is aware of the capabilities of the service provider. For something as complex as IT services it is also necessary to raise the awareness within the business of the potential of the product and this will involve high-level business analysis skills. By developing this understanding the agility of the services organisation increases in as much as the services provider will have an advantage over any competitor organisation in terms of time to market (or time to respond to the needs of the business) or indeed (in conjunction with sales) by preempting needs by proactively submitting plans for improvement.

If 'closeness to the business' is needed, what could be better to share with the business than an overview of the business and an agreement as to where the major opportunities for business improvement and IT investment lie?

Supporting this responsibility will be a budget large enough to provide the necessary skills, to ensure they can be deployed whenever necessary and to mount campaigns as and when necessary. This will clearly be greater during times where major change is anticipated.

Sales and value-add

Sales are clearly the lifeline of commercial organisations. For non-commercial enterprises we should still be concerned that there is a process for creating value because this is after all what all service organisations must deliver: nothing is purchased unless it is perceived to add value. Ambler (2006) talks about three stages of innovation corresponding to our sales activity: first the 'big idea', second the development of the big idea into a saleable product and finally selling the idea both internally and externally. We look specifically at sales strategy, sales management and the creation of business value.

Sales strategy

The scope of what a commercial IT services provider undertakes under the heading of sales will necessarily exceed that of an internal services organisation and so this section will describe the approach of the former and subsequently describe how this might be implemented by the latter. The business customer will judge how to interpret what behaviours they experience but both internal and external service providers must be seen to be behaving appropriately.

The service provider has few options to grow business. The first priority should be to retain and grow existing business which means lavishing lots of TLC (tender loving care) on current customers, then renewing contracts, increasing the transaction value, encouraging more frequent purchases, selling other things (cross selling) or attracting new customers through referrals. The next priority might be cold calls or desk research to reach new customers. The service provider must decide which of these it is to be or how much time is devoted to each group of activities and what targets should be set. Regardless of the preferred strategy, the actual proposals or investment cases will usually be aligned with the business objectives of the client organisation based on business awareness gained through market research, sales intelligence or other industry knowledge. Innovation and insight increase the value of proposals and may come from introspection but they more often come from exposing the business requirement to potential specialist suppliers and exposing the business manager to consultative selling techniques (which have more in common with consultancy methods than traditional selling techniques).

Using consultative selling to develop long-term relationships is a skill required of most sales persons in the business-to-business sector; they are all schooled to understand the value of retaining existing customers and the importance of developing repeat business. Coker et al. (2002) wrote about the customer hierarchy of expectation being at three levels: basic needs (product quality, reliability and trustworthiness), higher needs (problem solving) and highest needs (strategic problem solving). Miller et al. (1994) similarly describes five levels of the buy–sell relationship: delivering commodity that meets expectation, delivering 'good' product and services, providing 'good' service and support, contributing to business issues and finally contributing to organisational issues. The implication is that by moving up these levels the service provider can establish a long-term relationship.

All self-respecting service organisations will want to understand their potential customer. The research will often start with an organisation chart positioning the business managers, their roles and responsibilities and reporting lines. If there is a bid in prospect we also need to understand the interests of the business stakeholders with regard to the bid (e.g. sponsor, budget holder, business approval, other decision maker, technical approval etc.).

In the case of an existing customer a services provider would need to understand the current sources of revenue (the contribution matrix), the reasons for purchase, the needs and benefits and areas where there may be uncertainty or a lack of knowledge. Service providers would typically look for an inside salesman (or advocate) and would be looking to understand the personal as well as the business drivers in order to construct what might often be referred to as a 'win–win' situation. The researcher may also be the sales person during the research phase of the sales cycle or in larger organisations research may be a full time role.

All too often, existing customers look for reward. This can be in the form of a discount but that will ultimately inevitably bring a reduced service. Better then to look to reward loyalty in different ways, for example through some form of hospitality, by creating network opportunities, through free and useful PR or enhanced reputation, access to specialist skills etc. This is an area which is only limited by our imagination.

Sales management

Good sales management is always helpful to the customer. At worst business managers may feel that they are being sold to but they will also get access to information that can add value to the business. Some business managers do not take calls or emails from sales people and then either spend time trying to find out what is available or live in total ignorance of the latest developments. Being on the receiving end of high-quality sales campaigns can be illuminating. The interaction between a good salesperson and a good manager can be inspiring.

The professional IT organisation will research new prospects from their market analysis and plan their communications and operational budgets not just on what they are doing today but on what their sales forecasts are telling them. Forecasts will be updated frequently and be linked to the corporate planning process. These will be planned in conjunction with their marketing people to ensure that an integrated series of messages using mail (snail and email), calls, the media and events all deliver the same or complementary messages. Sales people will be organised in terms of product or territory. Time management is important to them and they are good at applying the Pareto principle, focusing on what will provide the best returns.

One of the key skills for any sales person is planning. The popular myth is that sales people are extrovert and risk-taking individuals. In fact they often have a technical background, are always very self-motivated and good at managing long-term and short-term goals. They maintain clear territorial responsibilities whether this is based on geography, accounts, segment, new business development or account management, telephone prefix codes or whatever. They maintain a systematic approach to their communication and will evaluate which mechanism is most appropriate in a given situation, but mostly they have a preference for face-to-face meetings: how else can you get immediate feedback on what you say? They take the time to correctly qualify business interest before providing more information or requesting more time from the business manager. Thus time at meetings or on the telephone is confined to useful topics that enhance the perception of their organisation and have the potential to add value to that of their business prospects (i.e. not just small talk). Ultimately as the selling organisation homes in on individuals who may have an interest in their solutions, sales people will be using diary management to ensure that they do not miss calls or waste time. Does your IT service provider treat you this well?

The commercial suppliers take this further with sales targets and a sales process designed to provide the service provider with realistic forecasts. They will develop value propositions around their products, services and proposals. These will be customer-focused and provide the business manager with a compelling reason to buy. This will usually be high in value-add to the business because that is the way the business case is established: no one ever buys anything unless the perceived value associated with the purchase exceeds the cost.

As the sales process proceeds the sales person will be making sure that key business stakeholders (or 'buying influences' as Miller et al. (1994) refer to them) have been identified and that they are all at the same point in the decision-making cycle. Rackham (1995) suggests a customer decision-making process of first recognising that change is needed or that needs are understood, that options have been considered, that concerns have been resolved, that a decision is ready to be made, that the customers have made the decision and are committed to the implementation of the solution. In the context of large business this is a complex process requiring a team rather than an individual and probably a team from the business customer as well. Dalrymple et al. (2001) refer to this as relationship selling; it differs from the traditional selling approach which is focused upon a single sales person and a single buyer, perhaps a purchasing manager or a CEO or CIO. Relationship selling embraces the higher levels of the buy-sell relationship referred to earlier under the heading of 'sales strategy'; it will establish multiple contacts between the service provider and the business customer. The information has to be gathered and stakeholders have to be managed; if one stakeholder is ready to make the purchase decision but the others are at some earlier stage of uncertainty then the decision-making process may fail. Sometimes a business clearly states its needs and goes out to tender from prospective suppliers. Where this requirement is less than clear then there generally follows a process to develop a detailed understanding of the required solution. Meetings will be held with stakeholders to understand the situation, to establish needs, to suggest solutions, and to understand the nature and scale of the benefits. Owing to the nature of this process it is often referred to as the consultative selling process. The final stages are referred to as the commitment process. If we fail to understand the consultative selling process we will usually fail to understand the requirement and the likely benefits. If we fail to understand the commitment process we usually fail to understand how we are to complete the sale (i.e. we must know who makes the final decision and what process must be followed).

As well as the selling processes there is also the selling document or the proposal. The proposal development in some organisations is an art form and yet others expect major decisions to be made on the flimsiest of evidence. Some organisations think that because they have the 'ducks in a row' as far as key stakeholders are concerned they do not need to worry about the proposal document itself. The whole sales process must be considered to be adding value not just for the vendor but also for the business. The final proposal is a part of this value-add process. It will contain the value proposition with the business case in a format ready for the investment submission. It is also the document that is passed around and handed to other key stakeholders who emerge during the decision-making process and who the salesman perhaps failed to meet or even identify. It becomes a means by which the business manager is able to become an advocate of the vendor: they become the inside salesman. As such service providers must treat the production of the proposal as a strategic exercise and budget for its production. Creative energies must be applied, it must conform to the service provider's house style (or the style guide) and thought must be given to such things as content, design and layout. Proposals should be distinctive and stand out amongst other documents. Alongside the proposal the commercial service provider may also have to manage the bidding process and if this is led by sales, the salesperson will need to draw upon the legal resources for contractual agreements. For some commercial service providers this can be an expensive process and not always a good investment so there will be a need to for the organisation to exercise judgement based on its view of its chances of winning. The cost of bidding can often exceed several millions of pounds and the final stages can become very competitive and sometimes be reduced quite literally to a Dutch auction where the lowest price wins the contract.

> The author recalls a UK sales and marketing director of a large services provider vetoing further price reductions in the final stages of a bidding process for a major outsource contract where there was just one other competitor. It pulled out of the bidding process but somehow this company failed to advise either the competitor or the business customer that it had decided to withdraw. The one remaining suppler continued to engage in discussions with the customer business and to reduce their price even further during the following week. When the last remaining 'competitor' had finished celebrating their 'win', they were subsequently committed to delivering their services for seven years and to incurring major losses. The business customer also had to deal for seven years with a supplier that could not afford to deliver a good quality of service within the terms negotiated.

The sales person may be incentivised to meet financial sales targets. Targets can be achieved by finding new customers or by selling more product or service to existing customers. Deriving more business value from existing customers is known in commercial circles as the 'widening process' and it is a role more often associated with farming rather than hunting. This is the domain of the account manager. Account managers are often regarded as heading the 'after sales' service to the business customer. Other titles for this role suggest the emphasis that may be given to the particular implementation: account director (maybe a senior member of the services organisation); programme director (if some kind of change is implied); and customer relationship manager (suggesting an emphasis on some kind of customer care programme). Everybody in a services organisation is aware of the importance of customers and everybody in the organisation has some kind of responsibility to the customer and in this sense can be considered to have a marketing role. If results are measured in terms of sales and sales targets are set, then these marketing roles become de-facto sales roles. It is important that everyone throughout the services provider organisation from the very top to the bottom consider themselves to be part of the marketing machine. Not everyone will be capable of selling; however the responsibility for selling must be clear. It is easy with internal services providers in particular for some people to lapse into a controlling or policing role where the emphasis seems to be on preventing things from happening rather than enabling them to happen. In these situations the business can be enormously creative at bypassing the IT services organisation, ultimately to the benefit of neither party. Senior management involvement in customer calls is essential and people in all roles should be given every opportunity to get exposure to the business. All IT suppliers, including internal IT service providers, have to add value and selling is the acid test (i.e. whether the value added is worth the purchase price). Few businesses are able to make any kind of investment without some kind of business case. This means that even internal IT service providers must have someone who is able to undertake the sales or value creation role. In smaller organisations the head of IT may take on this responsibility but in larger organisations there may be one or more account managers or business managers. The remit for these people varies and the extent to which they should be allowed to act in a true sales capacity will depend very much on the culture of the business in question.

Those of us that have any experience of major account sales strategies will know that an excellent way to gain the confidence of the business manager is to help them in turn to look after their customer. If a services organisation sells by creating value-add for its business customers, one valuable service it can provide is to find ways to improve the relationships between the business customer and its customers. Another way of improving relationships between the services organisation and the business is to deal efficiently and effectively with complaints or by making the business manager's problem your problem and using these situations as opportunities to create goodwill. In most cases where sales responsibilities are assigned to members of the management team of the internal services organisation, it is done on an informal basis. This means that objectives are at best soft, intangible or avoided and as a consequence there is little value-add for either the business or the services provider. On the other hand, formalise the responsibilities and the impact can be immense.

When British Rail was being privatised the internal IT services provider had to be transitioned such that it could survive in the private sector following a trade sale. The primary market was distracted by major structural change. Instead of one customer the service provider was rapidly moving to an industry model where it would have more than 100 different independent business customer organisations.

(Continued)

(Continued)

None of the people in the industry felt secure in their roles and none had the faintest idea of how the new industry structure would work (or if it would work). In addition the UK Government had restricted spend in the run up to privatisation and so any investment had to be found from existing budgets. On reflection this was not the easiest time to be establishing a radical cultural transformation of an internal IT services provider in the public sector. The services provider had a requirement for a marketing strategy, sales capability, sales collateral, a specialist consultancy team and account managers. The products were realigned to become more relevant to a privatised rail industry and then the culture was addressed to convince the people that they could be successful in a new commercial context. The change programme required excellent leadership and communications. It was necessary to be inclusive by involving as many people from within IT as wished to participate and we needed to demonstrate success. This was probably the largest and most successful transition of its kind that has ever been undertaken in any country. The service provider won major new contracts in the internal market worth several millions of pounds sterling as well as a large number of overseas contracts in the transportation IT market. In 1994 the IT services provider won the Computer Software and Services Association (now INTELLECT) award for Strategic Marketing.

Determining the business value of the sales process

The business buys because there is value to be derived from the purchase. This is true if we buy raw materials to turn into product, goods to resell or services that will save money, enable us to do things better or to do different things. We all want to claim the benefits of success but we must acknowledge the role of the salesman who will often be identifying and creating value-add investment opportunities for the business customer. The salesman knows that a buyer will need help to understand the value of their organisation's product or service and will be eager to work with the business to establish the business case. It follows then that this should be a key measure of the success of any sales activity. The same must be true of account management. Any attempt therefore to measure this, particularly where buyer and seller are able to agree on the numbers, would be immensely useful. In the absence of quantifiable benefits any assessment of the extent to which innovation and business value has been created by the IT services organisation during the sales process would be helpful. Often there is no attempt by either party to measure this and so we have to find a proxy for it. We can get an indication that there is value to the business and we can estimate the value to the service provider from the extent of repeat business, the average length of a contract, the size of the average order, the annual value of business, the number of referrals from the business and their annual value, the number of industry awards, media interest etc. Perhaps we can measure the effect of an initiative through the financial performance of the business since the implementation of the solution. It is often very difficult to isolate the causes of the changes in fortune of a business and often there will be more than one variable at any one time but some good pre- and post-implementation analysis can often separate these. It may not always be increased revenue, we may instead be measuring shifts in price or performance, maybe we can measure this directly in absolute terms or maybe we have to use benchmark comparisons to offset other changes. Perhaps we are looking at the reduction of risk or the elimination of some percentage of product failures where we can estimate the value with some confidence. Perhaps we assess the quality of the resulting investment portfolio (see the following section). However this is done we should identify the value of this creative and entrepreneurial early stage process as well as the value added by the delivery processes. In this way we are able to establish a baseline for any PIR. The potential to add value during these early stages is usually much greater than later in the service cycle, although of course ideas without delivery will be unacceptable.

Failure to measure the value that a professional sales process brings to even non-commercial organisations presupposes that all of the value eventually comes from those that deliver the solution. If this were to happen the service provider will only concern itself with the cost of sales or the sales value achieved versus targets. This could drive the services provider to arrive at incorrect conclusions about the value of the sales team.

Selling is a people-focused activity that requires sound business and product knowledge and excellent communication skills. The best sales people are aware of how their product or service can help their customer or potential customer, how their product or service compares with those of their competitors, how their customer or potential customer is positioned in their market, the technological developments within their market and where the customer stands in relation to other technical developments and are able to summarise this in a way that makes sense to the buyer in a relatively short time. This latter skill is the hardest of all. All sales people must be able to sell. The best can assess the needs of very senior and experienced business people and communicate the unique selling points of their product or service in an economical, convincing and engaging way. To a technician this may sometimes look as though the salesman is merely good at presentation; more often it is a result of detailed research, expert planning, a positive mental attitude, excellent business knowledge and management skills and an ability to engage with the customer or potential customer. Later in the sales cycle the sales people will need excellent negotiating skills, more research and planning, objectivity and the ability to handle objections or customer concerns. Throughout we will see professionalism.

At more junior levels we will often see these skills developing. Even on a telephone call we can differentiate the skilled communicator and the person who has bothered to research the business they are calling. The greeting, the introduction, the purpose of the call, the ability to listen and respond to the answers to questions and the ease with which a follow-up action is achieved all help to identify those who will succeed in more senior customer facing roles.

The investment portfolio and the sales pipeline

During the marketing process the IT services provider is seeking to understand the business requirement, develop the business need and raise awareness of the technical possibilities. During the sales process the services provider is proposing solutions, building the sales pipeline and helping the business to establish an investment portfolio and business case. The service provider of course may only be seeing a subset of the business investment portfolio or even a subset of the business IT investment portfolio.

Whether the service provider is focused on traditional sales processes associated with new business development or account management focused on increasing the spend by existing customers, there is a need to develop the sales pipeline. The sales pipeline is reviewed regularly and used to produce sales forecasts, to monitor, incentivise and reward the performance of the sales force, as input to the business planning cycle and to schedule delivery resources. The non-commercial service provider would do well to mimic this process, but placing the emphasis on the business IT investment portfolio to provide a focus for the value-add role of the service provider rather than just on sales value.

Whether we are viewing a sales pipeline or an investment portfolio we are seeing the planning interfaces between a service provider and the business. It will typically consist of further work packages, infrastructure investment, application solutions, change programmes and organisational development initiatives. There is usually a need to manage investment portfolios such that business requirements can be matched with potential solutions as money becomes available. The investments will be prioritised on the basis of perceived business impact, financial benefits, cost, dependency, business and technical risk.

Both the content and their characteristics will change over time so that periodically it will be necessary to update, review and reprioritise the portfolio. Many portfolios are not maintained in this way and consequently their value rapidly diminishes. They are created during some expensive strategy review and are then neglected until they become meaningless. In a volatile market the shelf life for a portfolio that is not being updated will be less than a year and because of the relentless progress of technology few are likely to be of any value after two to three years.

The major benefit of maintaining an IT investment portfolio as suggested is that an organisation is able to constantly assess the impact of any business change against the IT strategy and previously considered known schemes. In this way the business can often avoid unnecessary delays in responding to a new business requirement. The business is also more likely to be able to avoid poor investment decisions that may lead to point solutions, lack of integration, obsolescence and legacy that inhibit the agility of the business and dilemmas associated with balancing 'big' and 'little' business strategies etc. The service provider is able to consider the long-term requirement when making short-term investments.

Leadership in sales and value-add

The sales activities bring a service provider closer to its business customer. An investment portfolio or sales pipeline is tangible evidence of an aware and agile service provider that can deliver relevant value-add investment opportunities (i.e. opportunities that create value to the business). A healthy order book also means that resources can be scheduled more effectively.

The leadership responsibility for creating sales, adding value and securing repeat business must be clear. Usually this will be the sales and account management team but in the case of the non-commercial service provider these roles may not exist. In their absence the dynamics change and there is a real risk that there will be a lack of innovation, a lack of value creation in the relationship between the service provider and the business and hence a decline in the fortunes of the service provider in the business areas where the relationships are weak. Even in non-commercial organisations these responsibilities must be assigned if not in name then by virtue of the leadership role and the outcomes. There must also be a budget that adequately supports the sales activities of the service organisation.

Commercial, financial, legal and administrative

This is not supposed to represent the domain of any one director or manager but rather all of the activities that enable the organisation to understand that it is performing legally and profitably. Each task might be the domain of the chief financial officer (CFO), the company or corporate secretary or some other person but all together they have been divided into two areas for the convenience of the assessment: (i) commercial and financial management and (ii) legal and administrative.

Commercial and financial management

We can include here everything in the financial management lifecycle from forecasting (income and expenditure), financial planning, cost and availability of investment capital, cost justification, investment decisions, financial management, the accuracy and quality of financial reports, cash flow and age of debt, the definition of what is a cost or profit centre, responsibility accounting, the identity of cost elements, activity analysis, activity-based costing, operational costs, fixed costs, unit costs, direct costs, variable costs, indirect costs, marginal costs and depreciation. It could include time sheets and job costing. There is the matter of taxation and the whole area of taxation accounting and the effects of taxation on profit and cash flow. This can be further complicated for multinational businesses where there are the challenges of international trade, international financing and exchange rates to worry about; this has to be balanced against the opportunity of deciding where to borrow (interest rate implications) and declare profit (taxation implications). International companies sometimes establish internal conversion rates to simplify the trading relationship when moving stock or services between offices. These can be set for an extended period to create a predictable trading environment. We need to understand how capital allowances can influence these considerations. Finally there are the issues of financial stability, about books of accounts and of financial reporting.

Then when all of this has been considered we need to remember the effects of inflation and indexation. Being an economist can be helpful although each economist seems to have a different view of both what is happening and the causes.

If we have a commercial interest then we can add profit or profit margin, sales pipeline, pricing, price and volume calculations, differential charging, pricing flexibility, contractual agreements, general terms and conditions, risk-reward contracts, billing and the billing cycle, profit and loss accounting, VAT returns and balance sheets. There are the statutory accounts to be filed and the auditor's reports to deal with. Accounts are expected to be filed on time and this boosts investor confidence.

If we have an investment interest then we can add payback and net present value, shareholder value added, investment cost, cost and availability of capital, opportunity cost, internal rate of return, risk-adjusted discount rates and ROI. Project accounts are a combination of financial and management accounting with specific interpretations (e.g. earned value). We may have to consider cash flow, cost distribution, stage payments and performance or retention bonds. If investment is project related, project accounting may be part of the project office responsibilities, there may be an accountant assigned to the project or the project or programme manager may take responsibility for managing the financial aspects. If assets are not purchased using capital they may be leased or hired creating leasing decisions and issues around the financing of leases, taxation and leases, sale and leaseback, leasing versus hire purchase, operating leases, residual value, exchange leases etc. Finally we may become focused on the exit strategy, especially if we have attracted venture capital.

Instead of making an investment we may be interested in outsourcing and so we will be looking at the cost reduction opportunity or even asset renewal and service improvement. If we are a business customer it may be all of these things.

In all cases there are the management accounting dimensions: the issues about budgets and performance reporting against budget, budget responsibility, the quality and level of detail of information available and the quality and level of detail required. Regardless of what kind of business we are involved in managing, we and our customers need to be confident that we are able to use our financial and management information effectively both up and down the management chain and across the supply chain and to our customers at the point of delivery: the end-to-end process. Invoice integrity can be a big issue; customers must not be lost because charges are unclear or because there is a lack of confidence in the validity of the charges being levied. Where there is a cost allocation or apportionment of part of the cost of a service to a customer and this is perceived not to be realistic by any key stakeholder then this creates a feeling of distrust. This can apply equally to both commercial and internal service providers.

Do we have a well-defined critical information set? Do we set targets, manage KPIs, identify and deliver according to critical success factors, manage by key ratios or use a balanced scorecard approach? Do we measure the progress of each project and process and do we have good controls and success criteria for the outcome of each process? Are these a part of our business and project planning process? Perhaps these are validated using some kind of benchmark comparison. Perhaps the benchmarking is built into the planning cycle. Hopefully the main cost and revenue drivers have been identified, are understood, are reviewed regularly and are tracked. These cost and revenue drivers could include salaries and the cost of employment, NPD or research and development, the cost of acquisition of a new customer, capital investment in plant and machinery or IT service delivery costs. Hopefully this detail will remain hidden to the business customers until that is some aspect becomes a cause of concern to them (e.g. incorrect billing, inadequate information, an apparent lack of internal cost control, late filing of accounts, poor forecasting resulting in under-resourcing etc.).

So it is not just about gathering information and meeting statutory requirements, but about providing meaningful information to those with financial responsibilities for any aspect of the service provision. It is about enabling everyone in the service organisation to do their jobs effectively and efficiently and most importantly it is about ensuring that there is no loss of confidence amongst the customer community.

Legal and administrative management

A company secretary (sometimes referred to as the Corporate Secretary) ensures that an organisation complies with relevant legislation and regulation and keeps board members informed of their legal responsibilities.

It is also their responsibility to register and communicate with shareholders, to ensure that dividends are paid and to maintain company records (lists of directors and shareholders and annual accounts).

It is not a legal requirement in the UK for all service providers to employ a company secretary unless they are publicly owned companies (i.e. PLCs). As regulation increases however the role could become a model for dealing with governance structures, board, shareholder and trustee meetings, compliance with all regulatory, legal and listing requirements, the training and induction of non-executive directors and trustees, dealings with regulatory and external bodies, communication with shareholders and trustees, the management of employee benefits (e.g. pensions, employee share schemes), insurance administration and organisation and the interpretation of the financial accounts.

The larger commercial service providers frequently have access to a full-time legal council or barrister specialising in the more obvious cases of litigation that the organisation will be exposed to. Other service providers will be advised to recognise the growing requirements for legal compliance and assign responsibility accordingly.

Figure 3.13 illustrates the growing legislative framework requiring compliance in the IT sector. It allocates the various legal frameworks to the ITDYNAMICS™ assessment framework for the service engine to show where the impact is most likely to be felt.

Figure 3.13 shows how the legislation embraces all activities from marketing to final delivery of the products, services and the licenses for the deployed technology. We must include intellectual property rights (IPR), such as confidentiality agreements and access agreements, the registration of brand names and trademarks, the administration of privacy and data protection. Our relationships with suppliers, customers and employees are all under scrutiny. Useful references for law include Holt and Newton (2004) for an IT perspective or Kolah (2002) for a broader perspective. The whole organisation must be aware of the risks, the responsibility for compliance and for making sure that everyone is aware of their legal responsibilities and these must be clearly assigned within the organisation.

The area where finance and the commercial and administrative processes might overlap are those to do with the setting of objectives, where business strategies and plans are developed and budgets set and where the major objectives for divisions and departments that support the strategy are developed. Unit managers collaboratively set specific objectives for their units with their superiors; specific objectives are set collaboratively for all departmental members. Action plans to deliver objectives are specified and approved. Action plans are implemented. Progress toward objectives is monitored and feedback provided. Successful achievement is reinforced by performance-related pay or rewards.

	Contract law	Employment law[1]	Intellectual assets[2]	Data and privacy laws[3]	E-commerce directives[4]	Behavioural laws[5]	Defective product	New Companies Act, SOX	Competition law	Industry-specific legislation[6]	Computer misuse	Environmental laws
Business and sector awareness										√		√
Marketing and communications				√	√	√						
Sales and value-add	√					√	√					
Commercial, financial, legal and administrative	√	√	√	√	√	√	√	√	√	√	√	√
People, organisation and governance		√				√					√	
Product and service definition	√		√			√	√			√		√
Product and service delivery	√		√			√	√			√		√
Bought-in products and services	√		√			√	√			√		√
Security			√	√	√							
Technology			√	√								√

Notes:

[1] For example the Health and Safety at Work Act.

[2] For example intellectual property rights, copyright and performing rights.

[3] For example the Data Protection Act, European Privacy Directive, California's Security Breach Notification Act 2003 and California Online Privacy Protection Act 2003 (OPPA).

[4] For example the Electronic Commerce Directive, Electronic Signatures Directive, Electronic Money Institutions Directive and Privacy and Electronic Communications Directive.

[5] For example libel, defamation, deceit or misrepresentation.

[6] For example the Freedom of Information Act and food traceability.

FIGURE 3.13   *Scope of legal frameworks*

There is also a huge administrative underbelly of trivial administrative activity associated with travel arrangements, company car provision, expenses accounting, catering, meeting room administration, telephone directories, credit card bills and payments, pensions administration, medical insurance and healthcare and so on. These often become a distraction to any company and the cost of providing these services can be under-estimated.

As with all of our management dimensions, we have to ask questions about what we are spending on managing these various overhead aspects of the IT services organisation and what we are getting in return for this expenditure. We have been looking at the tremendous scope and complexity of the financial portfolio for an IT services organisation and we must be sure that it is being satisfactorily executed, even though (or perhaps because) the head of IT may often report to the corporate head of finance. The author has witnessed ineffective planning, poor management, inadequate accounting controls, bad financial systems support and non-existent reporting. There was the major services company that used a spreadsheet for accounting and had not filed accounts for three years. There was the public sector organisation that demanded cost reductions from its suppliers and would not pay supplier invoices for up to three months and yet had no internal controls on staff overtime or overtime payments. There is perhaps nothing worse than poor or even average fiscal control because it frustrates all attempts by management to improve the performance of the organisation.

Leadership of commercial, financial, legal and administrative

To many organisations, regardless of who undertakes these duties, these are all considered to have one thing in common: they are all overhead activities. Interestingly they are the activities that can cause the most pain and inconvenience for both the service provider and the business. Reassuringly, they are also areas where businesses will assume that they will not have a problem until that is one arises. Just as technical problems can be immediately visible at all levels of the business, so too can commercial, financial, legal and even administrative issues arise. This is an area that is only relevant to a business customer when it goes wrong, but nothing is likely to distance a business from its service provider more quickly or undermine business confidence more than failure in this area.

This is an area that is worthy of attention and clear leadership is important; where it comes from matters not and it will depend upon the organisation and the professional qualifications of the individuals concerned. The leadership of each aspect may be different, just so long as all four aspects are covered.

'Closeness to the business' is more interesting. Consider the service provider that has well-developed controls and reporting capabilities. Most businesses will be well catered for and their information needs well anticipated. Consider as well the IT services provider that makes this a part of its product augmentation and approaches its business community as an integrated part of itself by ensuring that the requirements in this area become an integral part of the business reporting routine. How close is that?

People, organisation and governance

Whatever we do and however we do it we influence what people think about us simply by virtue of who we are and how we conduct ourselves. It has been said that people buy from people, that we associate with like-minded people and that we only do business with people we like. This is often influenced by national and cultural differences and if this interests the reader it will be worth referring to Harrison and Huntingdon's (2000) research into the relationship between trust and economic performance. Not only do we need to be able to trust people we deal with but in professional circles in particular there is plenty of evidence to suggest that we probably need to respect the experience, ability, professionalism and the personality of those that we will choose to help us. This will influence how we organise ourselves and relate to others.

The organisation structure

The organisation chart is the most common way of defining roles and reporting lines. Without more detail it will often merely give us a clue as to the responsibilities. On the other hand we can get a feel for the breadth and depth of responsibility from the shape of the chart. Is it flat, does it reveal clear and effective reporting lines, are job titles meaningful with transparent responsibilities, does it tell us what is outsourced or subcontracted, can we get an understanding of the ratio of full-time staff to part-time and temporary staff? Responsibilities often separate specialist knowledge from the management of people. Each could carry large budgets. For example we may see responsibilities for planning and strategy, infrastructure management, business applications, information management, information security, supplier management, customer support or support services, major technology driven change programmes and, in commercially oriented organisations, research and development, NPD, sales and marketing. It is reasonable to expect each department to have its own objectives and critical success factors. How we organise these roles, assign responsibilities and set objectives is going to influence relationships but will tell us little about how the organisation functions and so this must be understood more fully. Just as it is useful to the service provider to have an organisation chart of the business, it is useful for the business to have an organisation chart of the service provider.

Governance framework

Even if we understand how roles and responsibilities are distributed we also need to formally define the manner in which the big decisions are taken. In the past this would have focused on the size of the IT budget, then later on the amount of investment being made in technology as a result of strategy and planning work undertaken by the service provider to the business. We are talking about how the IT services provider is managed and how the IT services provider manages the business. It is about how investment decisions are debated and agreed. We need to know who is responsible for what, but we may also wish to exert influence over IT investment, procurement and recruitment policy: we must decide how much we wish to spend on IT (the capital and revenue budgets), influence how that will be spent (improved performance or service levels, up-to-date infrastructure, new applications etc.), whether there should be any attempt to recover the costs according to use and how IT is to be aligned with the business units and their processes. Where we have choice we need to manage investment priorities, decide what and when to outsource and perhaps ensure that corporate social policies are applied. The ITDYNAMICS™ assessment framework for the service engine is a useful structure for governance because it addresses all activities. Each of these must be subject to some form of governance for which someone might take responsibility. This is set out in Figure 3.14.

No	Title	Governance criteria	Business area responsibility	Service provider responsibility
1	Business and sector awareness	Understanding of the business' competitive and trading environment and the business strategy	All business management, corporate communications to brief service providers	All service provider management and staff
2	Marketing and communications	The service provider's interpretation of the business need; the communication of the capability	All business stakeholders	Marketing management
3	Sales and value-add	The relevance and added value associated with the proposed service or the IT investment portfolio and the communication of the commitment or investment process	Business budget holders, heads of divisions, purchasing department, other decision makers	Sales management
4	Commercial, financial, legal and administrative	Contractual agreements; the timeliness and accuracy of financial reporting by the services provider; the recovery of costs; the processes for settling financial transactions across the extended enterprise; legal compliance and administration	Business budget holders, buyers of services, CFO, purchasing department, company secretary	Financial, commercial, sales and account management and company secretary
5	People, organisation and governance	Service organisation and people dynamics, the growth and development of the workforce and matching this to the needs of the business customer	Business managers and staff having regular contact with the service provider	Board, all service provider management and staff
6	Product and service definition	Design of IT products and services and their suitability to the business in terms of functionality, linkage with external organisations, look, feel, ergonomics, warranties, extended credit, SLAs, ROI etc.	Process owners, budget holders	Sales management, business analysts, product development managers and service delivery management
7	Product and service delivery	Performance of IT in delivering new IT product (applications, databases, communications facilities etc.) and day-to-day service	Business change managers, responsible business managers, process owners, budget holders	Product development managers, service delivery managers and account management
8	Bought-in products and services	Appropriate sourcing of products from third parties by the services provider for reselling or subcontracting arrangements for services to increase the range quality of the services offered	Business budget holders, heads of divisions, purchasing department, other decision makers	Board, service definition and service delivery management
9	Security	The protection of the business from threats that can arise from security breaches or the loss of the IT infrastructure, breaches that can be introduced as a result of using an external service provider etc.	Board, business security officer, company secretary	Information security officer, sales, service definition and service delivery management and company secretary (if commercial service provider)
10	Technology	Technology made available to the business to exploit efficiencies and connectivity balanced against the realities such as ease of use and reliability	Board, divisional heads, business managers	Board, sales, service definition and service delivery management

Figure 3.14 *The ITDYNAMICS™ governance framework*

The governance style arising from the implementation of this or any other governance framework within a particular business will reflect the specifics of what has to be governed, the people available and the corporate management style. There are characteristic governance styles; according to the Sloane Business School these may be monarchic, autocratic, feudal, federal, democratic, anarchic and even arthritic. The governance mechanisms may then vary from the democratic-like mechanisms of executive committee, IT councils, architecture committee to the more autocratic methods of key accountable director, CFO or CIO. In the absence of any decreed mechanism or process everyone with a budget within a business will buy a point solution and every manager or employee in the service provision organisation that has money or resources will invent solutions to address perceived needs. The general comment here is that all businesses are different and so roles may vary but controls will come about one way or another and it is much better to have some form of planning than a free for all. Those who have the responsibility in the larger businesses will wish to involve others in order to extend their reach. The CIO in these circumstances will wish to be involved as extensively as possible given the modern context for IT. They will create forums, attend existing formal and informal business-focused and IT-focused gatherings and generally seek as much airtime as possible in order to seek feedback on services, seek input to strategy development and to communicate strategy.

Some of content of the governance framework suggested in Figure 3.14 is worthy of specific comment. Business management and the buyers of IT services expect IT services providers to be as well informed about the business and the business sector as they are themselves. Where there is an ongoing relationship or where the contract is large enough the business may wish to involve the corporate communications people to brief the services providers. It might be a good idea to invite corporate communications to arrange regular briefings for the management and staff of service providers and for them to be well connected with other groups and individuals responsible for IT governance to assess how well the briefing is feeding back through other IT activities (e.g. in strategy, systems design, service delivery etc.). The key objective from all of this communication is to raise business awareness and to provide a common direction for product and service definition and delivery. The business awareness dimension is complemented by the marketing and communications activities of the services provider. This is the means by which the services provider makes the business aware of its capabilities in terms of its products and services. All too often this is focused on a very narrow group (i.e. those who will eventually buy). In fact the decision-making process is far more complex in most businesses and it is very helpful if all stakeholders at many levels are aware of the products, services and reputation of the service provider so that buyers can get endorsement from their peers before a 'shortlisting' or purchase decision is made. Success at business awareness and marketing and communication will yield benefits to both parties at all levels but will probably be better assessed at the highest levels (i.e. at the board or executive level) because it is only here that it is truly possible to take a cross-organisational or non-partisan view.

The sales activities become much easier if the forgoing activities have been undertaken and were successful. The sales process is about identifying the value that is being created by the offer to provide product or service and so persuade the buyer to enter into a financial transaction to purchase the benefit stream associated with the investment. This sales or value-add activity will therefore be focused on the budget holder or divisional or business unit level where the benefits associated with an investment have to be considered. The impact of a poor sales process is that the financial or other information necessary to support a business case is not made available to the decision maker and as a consequence they may not invest and will have to forgo the benefits associated with the investment. The service provider will also have to forgo the income from the sale. There are always significant risks that all sales personnel will identify with when they have to sell to a purchasing department instead of directly to the business manager. Purchasing managers neither own the business problem nor the benefit stream resulting from the investment. The risks will always be seen to be high because procurement departments are often too far removed from the business, rarely understand the markets they operate in and are seen as middle men. The main consequence of this is that they frequently fail to recognise the value of features of the product or service to the business unless they are already listed as requirements. Hence all too often we see procurement people reviewing products or solutions against a checklist of requirements with little understanding of the consequences or the benefits associated with competing solutions. The risks can be reduced by engaging business managers in marketing and communications initiatives to raise awareness of products and services and ensuring that product or service features are shortlisted and through their involvement in relationship and consultative selling activities.

The 'commercial, financial, legal and administrative' heading appears to be a catchall for those activities which are tangential to the core product or service but which are key in terms of defining what is being delivered, at what cost, under what terms and in compliance of which laws. These will necessarily become the responsibility of different parties as the commercial arrangement develops and there will be a lifecycle of activity which follows the natural lifecycle of the contract. This will first involve the sales people from the service provider and buyers of the business. It will lead on to develop the nature of the relationship with the business budget holders, buyers of services, CFO, any purchasing department on behalf of the service definition or service delivery managers (or direct with them) and the company secretary. In most organisations the response from the service provider will be managed by the account manager assigned to the business in question who will have access to other specialists as necessary.

Wishing to avoid any circular arguments about the governance of governance, the people area is now most important in order that we can establish responsibilities and clear lines of communication. Depending upon the nature of the relationship between the parties it may be helpful to develop a common culture which leads to trust between business and service providers. The question arises as to who should take the responsibility for this. In fact it must be the collective responsibility of both parties. Both organisations stand to benefit from the relationship and so this must be an issue primarily at the highest level. An acid test is the frequency with which both management teams come together and under what circumstances. For large service contracts, team building should be undertaken at all levels in the relationship for the common culture to flourish so that the benefits can be maximised by both parties.

Product and service definition is not visible at high levels in a business but more realistically at the process owner levels; the people who are using the system on a day-to-day basis will know how well it has been designed or implemented. Early engagement with the people at these levels will always bear fruit, even if we are talking about training or developing expectation rather than radical product design.

Product and service delivery problems will be noticed by business change managers who are leading IT-enabled change and who are thus dependent upon the timely delivery of new solutions and also by responsible business managers who require services from IT in order to manage their part of the business efficiently and effectively. Both groups will require performance measures which will tell them how well delivery is proceeding.

Service providers who choose to buy in products and services will do so in order to broaden or improve their offering to the business. This may increase capability, create a new income stream or both. This practice is commonplace. In the product area vendors will have arrangements to ensure that resellers are seen to be approved resellers. In the services areas the arrangements are often less obvious although it is good practice to make it clear to those buying the service where a subcontract arrangement exists, the nature of the relationship, how it came about and how long the parties have been working together etc. This process should be designed to enable the buyer to put the same degree of trust into the relationship as the service provider and the subcontractor.

Organisations that have a corporate security officer should ensure that this person takes responsibility on behalf of the business for considering all security aspects. This will include assessing the risks, impacts, controls and the need to maintain business continuity. Responsibility for legal compliance in most organisations lies with the company or corporate secretary. The company secretary is responsible for making the company aware of its legal obligations. The IT service provider will probably be responding to both the business security manager and the company secretary and in turn advising both through its specialist information security officer. The governance of any compliant product must be managed throughout the product or service lifecycle from definition or design through to delivery by the product supplier and subsequently during use. This is a requirement with devices and systems that must conform to rigorous security or other national and international standards (e.g. medical devices). In the future this requirement is likely to spread to IT products and services in other sectors (e.g. in the financial services sector, the military, legal etc.).

Many will be surprised at the responsibility for the actual technology deployed to the technical platform. The CIO will have strong views about what should be deployed and for decisions taken in this area but we have to balance these views with those who might be most affected in the business. Where inappropriate decisions have been taken about an investment in technology it is usually the divisional head or the business unit manager who is most vocal because it is they who will know when their business is uncompetitive, when they have poor connectivity with the market or suppliers and when equipment or systems are unreliable or difficult to use.

To implement any governance model there is a need to define the roles and responsibilities and the relationships between the elements of governance as described above. The health of the IT in an organisation will be dependent upon the governance model and so there is a need to ensure that it is complete, coherent and is working effectively. A great solution is to appoint a non-executive director with the specific responsibility for alignment pulling together a picture of IT in the business, reporting to the board on a regular basis, making recommendations for corrective action and making any changes to the governance arrangements. This can be far more helpful than either a CIO defending what is clearly not working or spasmodic consultancy assignments followed by the punishment of the guilty and the reward of a lucrative reengineering contract for the perpetrator of the report. The alignment process could potentially draw upon many of the techniques used here including the ITDYNAMICS™ service excellence model, the ITDYNAMICS™ assessment framework for the service engine, as well as the ITDYNAMICS™ governance framework.

Corporate culture

Regardless of the organisational structure, the corporate management style and the governance framework, we must be conscious of culture. We use culture to refer to the less tangible characteristics that help to describe an organisation. It might describe behaviour, attitude or values.

It is sometimes revealing to ask people what words they would use to describe the organisation that supplies to them or that they are a part of. Let us take a look at some of the words that the author has heard being used.

- Service driven
- Customer-focused
- Positive, 'can do'
- Project oriented
- Responsive
- Flexible
- Quality
- Investors in people
- 'World class'
- Stimulating
- Resilient
- Professional and mature
- Achieve or leave
- Disciplined
- No blame

- Political, other agenda
- Bureaucratic
- Reactive
- Inflexible
- Impersonal
- Complacent, excuses
- Autocratic
- Just for profit
- Hire and fire
- Intellectual snobbery
- Yielding
- Incompetent
- Dead men's shoes
- Like herding cats
- Low risk: 'play the game'

- Stimulating and fun
- Transparent
- Clear accountabilities

- Low enjoyment
- Hidden objectives
- Unclear accountabilities or obfuscation

- Participative and consensus driven
- Clear direction and expectation
- Seeks consensus
- Others

- Autocratic

- Confusion reigns
- Cannot make decisions
- Others

You will see that these have been categorised almost as 'good' and 'bad' but it is often not that clear and the perception of a cultural value can say as much about the subject as it does the organisation. In fact these descriptions came from only about five or six assignments and in most cases there was little consensus.

It is interesting to research the many ways in which the management gurus describe and classify corporate cultures. We have included a few here to provide a flavour of what might be found. The theory of change quadrants aids organisational change by determining whether an organisation is cold or warm and whether the change is cold or warm. Cold organisations adhere to structure, rules, procedures etc. rather than shared values. Cold change is driven by an objectively discernable threat such as a takeover or competitive pressure rather than ambition. The idea is not to impose warm change on cold organisations or cold change on warm organisations. Quinn and Rohrbaugh (1983) devised a framework for organisational effectiveness around a three-dimensional model using internal versus external organisational focus, flexibility versus stability of the organisation and process versus outcomes orientation. In Handy's (1996) *Gods of Management,* Apollo represents a role culture driven by logic, authority and order, Athena represents a task culture driven by problem solving, expertise and respect, Zeus represents a club culture driven by intuition, control and money and Dionysus represents an existential culture driven by new experiences, one-to-one management and personal freedom. Geert Hofstede recognised national or ethnic traits when he developed his cultural dimensions (see http://www.geert-hofstede.com/). He suggested a framework for understanding and dealing with national and cultural differences that consisted of five cultural dimensions. These are: power distance, uncertainty avoidance, individualism versus collectivism, masculinity versus femininity and Confucian dynamism. Berenschot uses the seven forces model (Claus 1991) to describe the forces that make things happen. These include necessity, vision, success, spirit, structure, capabilities and systems. They are most powerful when used in combination to address differing aspects of a change. One that will particularly appeal to those with a left-brain bias will be the purposive change model developed by ten Have et al. (ten Have 2002; ten Have et al. 2003). Here organisational change is seen as the product of four processes: direction, consistency, coherence and feedback. Perhaps our favourite is the neurotic organisation devised by Kets de Vries and Miller (1991) which suggests that neurotic styles influence the organisational focus: paranoid organisations prefer a control structure, compulsive organisations use standardisation and control systems, dramatic organisations prefer a primitive structure to pursue new ventures and growth, depressive organisations like formal routines but hierarchy without leadership and schizoid organisations are merely political playgrounds. There are probably as many academic views of corporate culture as there are opinions by economists on government policy and clearly no standard way of describing such a thing. Being conscious of the possibilities however can be enormously helpful to those of us who wish to bring about change and there is another and more important implication that we must be aware of concerning the use of method and structure.

The IT sector relies heavily on methodology and structure. We tend to impose structure in the belief that this helps us to deliver complexity more successfully. From what we have just seen, we now know that if we try to impose methodologies onto organisations that do not operate using structure and logic we may have difficulties. Being able to recognise the strengths and weaknesses of the corporate culture and the management styles in use in an organisation is important. The fact that there is no consensus about how corporate cultures should be classified is not important; being aware that there are many different styles and only around 50% will adapt readily to structured methods (and as many again will not) is much more interesting. Imagine trying to use PRINCE2 in a schizoid organisation, in a Zeus culture or in an externally focused, goal-oriented organisation where extreme flexibility is preferred. Finally we must also recognise that many believe that businesses can be inhibited from improving by being stuck in an overly ordered state. Some would argue that these organisations need to bring more chaos into their management culture; in fact what generally happens is that they switch from a total process fixation to once more placing value on outcomes.

Changing or influencing the culture

Although for a large contract it is helpful to achieve a common culture across a business–service provider relationship in order to establish shared values and trust, there are times when cultural change is absolutely necessary. There are many ways in which the culture can be influenced or even changed quite dramatically but there are a number of common denominators: first-rate communication, time, a reason for the organisation to change and the existence of the catalysts for change.

The reasons will be many and varied but the strongest reasons are threat and greed. Unfortunately the reason will usually contain some kind of threat to the jobs of employees. Things such as changes to the market, competition, takeover, outsourcing and insourcing, offshoring and onshoring, technology or new regulation probably rank amongst the greatest threats. Faced with these very negative threats, morale will suffer and staff will look at their options (and look for leadership in these situations).

The catalysts for change fall into four major categories and they are generally used in combination.

- **Leadership to provide directional improvement**
  + Vision
  + Improvement programme
  + Goal setting
  + Global continuity and consistency
  + Best-in-class specialists
  + Motivation
  + Attitude
  + Empowerment
  + Role definition
  + Flexibility of structure to recognise peaks and needs
  + Group cohesiveness: alignment of group and organisational goals
  + Conflict-resolution approaches: assertiveness versus cooperativeness
  + Improved morale

- **Skills and learning to provide intellectual improvement**
  - ✦ Job enrichment
  - ✦ Performance assessment
  - ✦ Identification of training needs
  - ✦ Nationally recognised qualification
  - ✦ Identification of skills gaps
  - ✦ Technical development
  - ✦ Professional development
  - ✦ Personal development and career counselling or coaching
  - ✦ Recruitment of known specialists

- **Reward to provide financial improvement**
  - ✦ Salary versus competition and comparable positions
  - ✦ Share options
  - ✦ Bonuses and performance-related pay
  - ✦ Days away
  - ✦ Days off

- **Lifestyle improvement**
  - ✦ Working environment
  - ✦ Encourages communication
  - ✦ Paperless and tidy work environment
  - ✦ Team groupings
  - ✦ Involvement
  - ✦ Display areas
  - ✦ Rest areas
  - ✦ Lighting
  - ✦ Noise abatement initiatives
  - ✦ Access
  - ✦ Location
  - ✦ Reduced hours
  - ✦ Home-working

When we have developed the change programme using a reason and catalysts we need a first-class consistent, compelling and multi-dimensional communications strategy and a change manager to deliver them.

> The author was recently working as a change manager or interim CEO. The task was to transition a services organisation from one that did as it was bid (some of the time) to one that was proactively contributing to corporate strategy, policy and success. We pointed to the declining revenue stream and rising costs. We developed a vision, a new management structure, job descriptions were revised (jobs were evaluated to
>
> *(Continued)*

(Continued)

introduce grades and a nationally consistent salary structure), we brought in some new people, made some redundant and promoted others. The office accommodation was reviewed and an accommodation strategy was introduced designed to use space and people more effectively. We established an agenda for change and brought in a new IT services provider with more capability to enable the organisation to introduce the changes more quickly. Working groups were established in order to extend the involvement of the key people during the transition phase. A new governance structure was introduced to align the organisation with the needs of the shareholders and to provide continuity of purpose and direction. Finally we brought in a new CEO to consolidate the transition and to take the organisation forward. This was a classic example of reason and catalysts used in combination to achieve cultural change.

Group dynamics

Not long ago HR or personnel departments were subjecting anything that moved to psychometric testing to discover the natural traits of management and staff. Joiners were similarly assessed. This was very popular when HR was a powerful force at the board table. They had risen as a power base during the 1970s when manufacturing was king and companies employed large numbers of people. Their power rose still further in the 1980s and 1990s when organisations throughout the western hemisphere were downsizing, not because HR had found ways of making organisations more efficient but because IT had. Psychometric testing, amongst other techniques, enabled organisations to select the people who exhibited the characteristics they were looking for. Regardless of the stated intent the emphasis was usually much more on working out who could be released.

In group situations they aimed to build teams of individuals with complementary characteristics that would be more effective than teams that came together by chance. It was only occasionally successful; there was always a suspicion of process being substituted for outcome. The author has been a member of a group comprised of individuals with the same characteristics and instead of it being the disaster it was supposed to be, the group in fact functioned wonderfully well. These selection processes attempt to profile people by uncovering their basic characteristics such as skills types (e.g. artistic, written and spoken communication, practical, experimental, organisational, business, social etc.), aptitudes (e.g. acuteness, special recognition, numerical deduction, observation etc.) and personality traits (e.g. imaginative, spontaneous, deliberate, assertive, passive, gregarious, solitary etc.). Those who advocate this kind of analysis claim that certain combinations can predict team styles and that certain patterns can identify ideal job types.

Today appropriate skills, training and qualifications, experience, motivation, leadership, interests and interpersonal skills are considered to be much more important for group dynamics. Furthermore the team can further develop these through team working on live projects whereas, if we believe the psychometrics, personal traits cannot be changed. In a busy world shortcuts are frequently used; there is more about shortcuts in the gentle persuasion section, but here we can simply say that people who are liked and respected will generally have an advantage in any selection process.

Coaching for individual and group effectiveness

Individuals must look to achieve their own objectives as agreed with management and they will usually be assessed by their manager on this basis at least once a year. In some organisations business customers will be approached for their opinions of an individual from the services provider during the assessment process. Perhaps the HR department runs assessment centres to compare individuals either during recruitment or subsequently to identify high fliers. However, we have to accept that we are in fact judged far more frequently, maybe on a one-to-one basis over the telephone or in face-to-face meetings. Maybe we are judged at larger events when we are presenting to, managing or otherwise trying to influence a group. It is a fact that we have very few people in IT who are able to influence individual business leaders let alone whole businesses and yet these are skills that can be learned; in many cases these skills are more powerful in business terms than anything that can be achieved technically. Every investment decision depends upon someone being able to persuade a group of decision makers to invest. Competent people must be enabled to maximise their effectiveness. We use coaching to focus on performance whilst mentoring may more broadly aim at enabling mentor partners to achieve their potential. Many of today's businesses are comprised of small numbers of highly skilled individuals, coaching and mentoring is usually far more appropriate than evaluation.

Either as individuals or as organisations IT services providers have tended towards placing the training emphasis on keeping up with technology. They have often ignored the many other business skills and so people in these organisations have become limited by what they know, limited in their outlook and so limited in what they can achieve. Coaching and mentoring as development tools can be a powerful alternative at all levels in organisations but if left too late it does not allow the mentor partner (person being mentored) to achieve anything like their true potential. Mentoring can have a long-term perspective or a short and focused objective and is best started during the earlier part of a person's career. Experienced mentors will help the mentor partners to identify skills that they were not aware of and to help them to develop in ways that would otherwise not occur to them. The mentor may also be providing the mentor partner with access to a new network of contacts, access to new skills and more awareness and development opportunities. Mentoring can make huge differences to career expectation and achievement. At an organisational level it can make a huge difference to the collective capability and the dynamics of an organisation. Used cross organisationally and between organisations in an ecosystem or extended enterprise it can create a closeness and singularity of purpose that will benefit all parties. Few organisations reach this stage of development but it is more common outside of the IT sector than within it.

Gentle persuasion: making friends and influencing people

We have already discussed the importance of good communications skills for the IT services organisation. Here we stress the need for individuals to develop great communications skills: probably the most important skills that an individual needs after the technical or professional skills that got us into the IT services organisation in the first place. Technicians will refer to these as soft skills so we sometimes refer to this as the art of gentle persuasion.

We must regard every group as an audience that either needs to be managed, with whom we need to build a relationship or who will make an important investment decision that will benefit our organisation. Gentle persuasion is about how an audience might be managed in order to achieve one of these objectives. If you have ever sat through a presentation or a meeting that had no focus or purpose then you will be aware of the scandal of the unfocused speaker. These people ask us to listen to them and then waste our time by failing to manage either their audience or their opportunity adequately. Every now and again it is worth reviewing the techniques we use for managing meetings and making a few improvements here and there. It is after all the way we influence people to look at things as we do or buy what we are selling.

Cialdini (2000) suggested that in this complex world business has developed shortcuts for decision making. The implication is that people do not work through the logic and the business case because there is no time; instead they will look for other indicators to decide how to act. He suggests that the speaker can use six shortcuts that would be recognised by business leaders: reciprocation, commitment, social truth, liking, authority and scarcity. Reciprocation means that by giving something the presenter creates a future obligation; commitment and consistency leads to repeated commitments; social truth is the public acknowledgement that prompts respect; liking is about making friends (to influence people); people respond to symbols of authority such as rank, titles, uniforms, power dressing, prestige cars, imposing offices, large houses and even horses; and finally scarcity increases value and desire, especially if there is competition. Hoar (2005) suggested nine techniques of persuasion: apply logic using facts, logic and argument; inspire by appealing to emotions describing end result; be inclusive by adopting a consultative approach; make the audience feel good by addressing their self-interest and leave the audience feeling positive about you; offer a deal, create a feeling of indebtedness; ask a favour by perhaps requesting a commitment that will repay later; name drop and so imply that there is endorsement; pull rank and so invoke power of status, rules, traditions or superior knowledge; and use force by using assertive behaviour, threats, warnings or FUD (fear, uncertainty and doubt) etc. There are clearly close similarities with Cialdini.

Many of our best opportunities to influence people are when we give presentations and yet we often fail to either plan properly or deliver effectively. The key learning points are grouped under the four Ps: purpose, plan, performance and personality.

Purpose, put simply, means that we must ask ourselves what we are trying to achieve and how we will know when we have achieved it. It is a good idea to have these fixed in our minds before we start to plan for presentations. All too often we regard presentations as a necessary evil and we go through the motions and are thankful when we have got to the end. How many arguments have been lost because we either failed to focus on our goal or continued long after we had already won the argument?

Plan means that we need to consider the expectations and needs of our audience. Their level of knowledge will determine how we pitch our argument; there may be constraints that have to be considered (e.g. we will only be given 30 minutes to make our case). We should not plan to put across more than five or six topics if our presentation is to have any clarity of purpose. As this will be delivered face to face, we must decide what style of presentation and what tone of voice would be most effective. Most presentations predictably use PowerPoint these days because this is an easy way to put across complex arguments and yet we ignore the opportunity to mix this with the face-to-face techniques of 'talk and chalk' (building the presentation interactively with the audience and charting key words on a flipchart or similar visual device), 'stand-up' (talking and interacting with the audience without any visual aids) and 'listen to me' (telling a story) styles of engagement. Regardless of the style we choose we must structure our presentation, just like a good book, by having an opening, a middle and an end. Finally our chosen 'tone of voice' will influence how we are received, such as being authoritative or intellectually superior, friendly or collaborative, professional or consultative etc.

The performance is the delivery of the presentation. The opening is an opportunity for the speaker to take the initiative, state the main thrust of the argument and set the scene for the middle or body of the presentation. We must be clear why we are there and put this across to the audience unambiguously. We must always take care if we choose to demonstrate superior knowledge because we will be amongst experts (at least of their own business). If we are not known to our audience we can always expect to be tested because they will want to know if we know our subject. We must quickly get the audience on our side, build a rapport and establish compliance (i.e. gain control). We must deal with interruptions. Interruptions mean that someone is expressing a strong opinion and this presents an opportunity to engage rather than pitch and yet it is an opportunity often wasted by a politician-like 'stock answer'. Not only do 'stock answers' not engage but they only work once. The middle must be orderly and logical (IT folks are not bad at this); keep to ideas that everyone will support or at least take care when introducing topics that may not have everyone's support; allow an appropriate amount of involvement but do not allow anyone to divert you (anecdotes can be a problem); maintain the relevance; take care with jokes (you may not be good at telling them, the audience may not be receptive at that moment or you may offend someone). At the end restate key messages and make sure you come back to the reason for your presentation. Always use pauses and modify the tone between each major topic. Finally be conscious of your body language, consider what you look like as you speak.

Let your personality shine through. When presenting be yourself, be different and be liked (that means do not patronise, antagonise or marginalise). People worry about being different, it is really OK to be different but it is essential that you are liked.

Success as always is best measured in terms of outcomes. Remember that the close comes not at the end but at the point where the purpose has been achieved. Make the close powerful (another 'P') or at least memorable. The acid test is whether you achieved your goal.

Not all of our presentations have major objectives, sometimes we are just informing, but we still need feedback. Many presenters circulate a questionnaire to get this feedback in order to determine whether the presentation met the listeners' needs or how they rated the presentation in terms of content and delivery.

IT is so critical and pivotal that failure to communicate can have a profound effect upon the fortunes of a business. Poor communication skills means that the service provider necessarily lacks business focus.

Leadership of people: organisation and governance

First-class leadership is an essential requirement in modern business. What do we mean by leadership? It may be about having market insight, showing thought leadership, being able to put together a compelling proposition, being able to close a sale, possessing leading edge design skills, leading from the front as a project, programme or change manager, managing a key supplier, having superior technical knowledge or perhaps it is about motivating others to do something they do not really want to do. As suggested here the kind of leadership required will be different in each of the skill sets in the assessment framework and in each major group of activities.

Already we are looking for someone to take the lead in each skill area but generally speaking there is an assumption that there will also be an overall leader, someone who is charismatic, powerful and persuasive and who operates at senior levels in the business. Actually it is often much more about circumstance: **cometh the moment cometh the man**. In times past leaders would have a long 'sell-by date' because there was little media exposure and so we would not tire of them so quickly. Today by comparison, leaders have to lead and are observed in more circumstances and we do notice that they sometimes under-perform. If you enjoy this kind of exposure you should invest in those around you to prepare you for meetings ensuring that you are well briefed and that you have rehearsed what you will be saying. Few of us are natural leaders and few of us can sustain long periods of exposure to scrutiny. The greatness of most leaders is in knowing when to cede to others, either because of the subject matter or because of the circumstances.

Leaders emerge: like cream they rise to the top. However some need a bit of help and someone has to take the responsibility of developing tomorrow's leaders. It is also important that employees take responsibility for their own futures.

Closeness can be enhanced by publishing an organisation chart for business consumption, by clear governance structures, by encouraging a culture that is openly consistent with what the organisation does and who it serves, by developing and using great communication skills and by cross-organisational mentoring.

Product and service definition

This aspect of service is the key to defining what is required, either for a new product or service or for a major change to an existing product or service. This may lead to the design of product and the planning of the infrastructure that will ultimately deliver service. Mistakes made during this phase are difficult to deal with economically later and can be the single biggest reason for a service requirement gap. Dissatisfaction always follows.

Within ITIL v3 this area is addressed by the service strategy (value creation, service assets, service provider types, service capabilities and resources, service structures, defining the service market, developing service offerings, financial management, service portfolios, demand management, service assessment and ROI) and service design (aspects of service design, service catalogue management, service requirements, service design models, capacity management, availability management and service-level management) processes (ITIL 2007).

Where do we start?

Most businesses would like to think that their IT service provider is going to take a structured approach to understanding what they need and this is probably the IT service provider's preferred approach. Beware though: some businesses can become frustrated by the chosen methodology and the IT service provider must look for any sign of this and consider alternative approaches in order to retain the interest and involvement of the business. Without this interest and involvement the outputs are merely the consequences of a process rather than the needs of the business.

Another common starting point is the solution-directed requirements planning process (i.e. where the sponsor already knows the answer before the analysis is complete). This is often the preferred approach from the business because it is solution-focused and the sponsor probably knows another business in the sector that is already using this solution and therefore knows how they may benefit from its use. Clearly the risk here is that the requirement is not adequately understood or the solution cannot easily be deployed in the business in question.

If a structured approach or method is used at any stage it should be in the hands of someone that has the experience to know when it is leading them astray, is sensitive to the needs of the business and is independent of the potential solutions providers. This can lead to a coherent strategy and a clear set of actions. From this we can define the infrastructure to support the requirement and select or specify the business solutions and services.

If the business has an immediate problem and needs some changes we often have to circumvent this neat and logical sequence. If we have been able to do our job properly we will already have some of the components in place; we may have a strategy, a portfolio of ideas that we have worked on and a major investment in infrastructure. We scope the changes and we identify any significant new requirement calling for a new business solution. We may have some big challenges: do we buy or build, does the preferred solution fit with our current infrastructure investment, how does this impact on the strategy? The business will wish to move forward quickly to put a solution in place but the IT service provider will want to be sure that it understands how it all comes together.

In this latter scenario the IT services provider can often be seen to be inhibiting the business from moving forward. It cannot delay progress but it must provide a working solution. There are people who will need to understand the requirement more fully and to understand how the new requirement integrates in business terms with process and existing solutions, there will be others who will be tasked with working out the detail of what solution would be most appropriate, the testing strategy, the approach to implementation or deployment, the operational require-ments, support issues and service levels. All of this can be very frustrating if you are sitting on the business problem just wanting to maintain market share.

Mostly this kind of problem exists where there are major shifts in the market but it can be argued that they could have been anticipated.

If the scope of the strategic and business area requirements planning work had been more broadly based and involved those people who had a view of how the market might shift, then the requirement might have been anticipated and the solutions already in place may have been selected on the basis of a longer-term view. There will have been value to the business in just exposing it to the possibilities that the technology can bring to the business. There may already have been an investment item in the portfolio where the need had already been scoped out and vendors already identified. Perhaps the infrastructure had already been selected on the basis of the likely future requirements and therefore no further investment was necessary. In this situation the IT services provider would be in a strong position to respond quickly to the business and as a consequence would have been seen to be more relevant, agile and aware.

Understanding the requirement

The aim of any requirements planning phase or 'stake-out study' as it is sometimes called must be to derive a thorough understanding of the current business situation. This will be based on top-down and bottom-up analysis of current processes, transactions, documents, management papers, interviews with individuals or focus groups, inputs from other teams, projects and organisations (customers, suppliers etc.), asset registers and obsolescence plans. It may lead to corporate and business area IT strategies developed in an integrated way or with a frequent 'unify and align' process. There must be strong links to the business in terms of understanding, sponsorship and acceptance. It helps if the vision, key business drivers, objectives, critical success factors, critical information needs and critical information set etc. are clearly set out. There may be a high-level ('ebusiness') architecture showing key stakeholder groups, processes and applications (e.g. Kalakota and Robinson 1999). There should be good mapping of end-to-end processes integrating with suppliers and customers, perhaps showing a before and after state, and infrastructure plans incorporating the required features. Gaps will be identified and possible future solutions scoped out.

There will be regular checks of business and technical assumptions in all recommendations and plans to ensure that they are supported. There may be some scenario planning based on permutations of business opportunity perhaps with a distinction between 'big plans' and 'small plans'. It should lead to an easily understood portfolio of investment opportunity based on an honest assessment of costs, benefits, business impact, risks and dependencies and these will be built into the business plans and budgets as the ideas are adopted. As the portfolio develops it will present options providing a degree of choice in investment. There will be detailed scoping, planning and costing of any high-priority investment proposals. The scope of any proposed change will be well defined and the business and IT implications understood. There will be an open funding approval process leading to programme initiation and the establishment of an appropriate governance structure for each change programme. Those responsible for the planning processes will be eager to learn from PIRs in order to assess progress and future speed of investment.

Product and service design

This is often a great area of weakness for IT product and service suppliers. It is often a lost opportunity for the IT organisation and a period of disinterest from the business as IT focuses on process and technology. Let us contrast this with the way in which a commercially oriented IT software or services provider (hopefully) or a market driven product or services organisation in another sector would tackle the design phase.

Marketers have understood the need to add value to the core product for many years (see Figure 3.15). Marketers regard a product or service as having a core, a further layer called the actual product and the outer layer called the augmented product. There are many interpretations of what this means and so what follows is an interpretation for IT service providers.

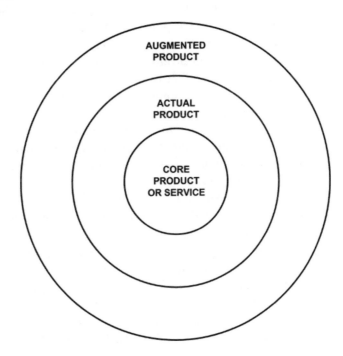

FIGURE 3.15 *Layers of a product or service*

The core product or service is all about what the product does for the business. It includes the technical platform, essential functionality, primary features, key design characteristics and attributes that the business customer will find necessary in the target market. For services it will address the ITIL v3 criteria. All too often this is where it ends. Mudie and Cottam (1993) describe the design elements as customer contact, service mix (i.e. the range of services), location of service consumption (i.e. where the service is used), design of service facility and accessories, technology, employees (number required), organisation structure, information (management information and who will have access), demand and supply management (demand patterns and supply flexibility, procedures (standardised or customised) and control (to ensure smooth running). The product surround (the two outer rings of actual product and augmented product) is designed to add value.

The actual product is more about look and feel. It includes branding, screen designs, compatibility and connectivity with internal and external services, contact with other user organisations and all of the additional features and product attributes outside of what might be considered to be essential. Novel features that can provide competitive advantage will be introduced as part of the actual product. These have a tendency to become part of the core product over time as competitors introduce the same feature and it becomes commoditised. Pricing will generally come under this heading until such time as the whole product is a commodity at which point it will may become a standard feature of the infrastructure and have no discernable price.

The augmented product must address the more practical concerns of access (product distribution), implementation and service support, service guarantees, financial security, financial assistance and futures. At the very least this will include the provision of source code by means of an escrow service to the business customer in the event of company liquidation but it should also consider installation services, warranties, after sales service, assumed future product enhancements, credit and financial arrangements etc.

It is important for IT products and services to be augmented in this way and that we take this into account when we assess an IT product, service or organisation. Product augmentation enables marketers to fully satisfy the broader needs of the customer and to introduce more possibilities into how they might improve the perception of what is delivered. By doing this they are able to address not just the basic business needs but also the emotional needs of the business customer. If we are describing service rather than product we may include our experiences of the ambience of the front office and the feel of the back office in the course of our encounters with the service provider. The product or service can be further augmented by the assistance or support that the service provider may offer in order to get the product or service to the business, the steps it will take to ensure that it is fit for purpose and the means of providing customer reassurance throughout the life of the product or service. This may include delivery or installation services, additional service-level guarantees, contracts or warranties, after sales support, customer service and service management, contact with other users of the product, credit terms etc. Finally, in this augmentation layer we may add the potential or perceived benefits of future upgrade paths. If these augmentation features are to have credibility with the business they should be straightforward, self-evident and unconditional rather than couched in jargon or small print. It is important that the customer develops a long-term view of the importance or significance of the product or the service. For this to happen the product must clearly be relevant to the business and have future-proof design features. It is an opportunity to make the business aware of the importance of the investment. Rather than a feature this may be future development, planned new releases and the value propositions these present to the business customer. Demonstrating how business users can contribute toward future releases encourages commitment.

Now here is the most interesting aspect of the product layers. When explaining how the differentiation of a brand is achieved by adding value to a basic core product Christopher et al. (1991) observed that the core, the essential elemental attributes, may represent 70% of the cost yet may have only 30% of the total impact on the customer. By contrast they observed that the surround may represent perhaps 30% of the costs but may represent as much as 70% of the total impact on the customer. The appeal then is in the product surround (i.e. the actual and augmented product). This means that we should not hold back when it comes to investing in the augmentation of the product or service or in adding to the emotional appeal of the product or service. So these are not optional add-ons: the businesses will expect them from all suppliers. The only issue to be questioned is what to include and at what cost. Understanding which features will add the most value to the business is key and will be determined through market research. If brand is important this augmentation will need to reflect the emotion that is the brand. All layers provide business features, quality issues, supplier capabilities, major benefits associated with the design or construction, the packaging, the brand and the peer pressure to use the product or service (i.e. who else is using it).

At the very least the product or service design phase presents the opportunity for the IT organisation to demonstrate how it can reduce overall costs to the business through either displacement or avoidance. Maybe it provides an opportunity for the business to achieve revenue growth, provide better management information, cater for increased volumes, reduce errors, improve competitive advantage, catch up on the competition or improve management control, productivity, staff morale, corporate image, customer service, customer relationships etc.

Build versus buy

It is now generally accepted that to build a solution is the last resort. This may have to be challenged as the technology moves forward but for the moment let us look at the reason for this received wisdom.

First we mostly have a rich infrastructure and if a problem requires a solution we may already have a feature of some software that is already installed that may not require further investment. This may be a desktop office solution or a little-known feature of enterprise resource management that has not so far been used by our organisation. Second we may be able to amend an existing application to give us what is needed. Third we may be able to enable an existing feature of a package solution; maybe we have the package but have to acquire a licence for the required new feature. Fourth we may be able to source a new package that does what we want. Finally we can just go and build it. We could construct a simple decision tree to reflect these choices. In general the decision will be influenced by our perceptions of the costs, benefits, impact, risk and dependency of the options (time to implementation will influence costs, benefits and impact). In most cases we would just take the cheapest and easiest option but as the solution becomes more complex then value plays a bigger part in the decision. If a new solution is being sought it comes down to a build or buy decision. It is easy for the IT function or the IT service provider to under-estimate the value of a function-rich product solution to the business. As a consequence we often see decisions taken to build based on an assumption that it is cheaper to provide just the functionality required rather than to perhaps spend a little more money to gain a lot more functionality. Few organisations can afford to build the same value into products that a vendor will do and hence the reason for including product layers into the discussion earlier. Most valid build decisions are made by large organisations and are based upon assumptions about competitive advantage (i.e. the value of having a unique solution).

Businesses value unique solutions and technology is adapting to this. As application generators become smarter and we can build intelligence into business process more quickly we may see a move away from packaged solutions but packages themselves are becoming smarter and more easily customised. We move relentlessly towards more automation of solution and service delivery with the focus becoming one of integration or orchestration of services.

Infrastructure planning

The concept of product design described above can be applied to anything. Take infrastructure, for example, something we all take for granted. The core infrastructure product simply has to support networked users with basic communications and access to common applications and data. Yet the infrastructure in some organisations is much better than it is in others. In some it appears that functionality and features have been removed as if to turn the clock back for the business users of those systems; these businesses are being denied access to the features that can make the business more effective. Others look at the business requirement and put together the features and technologies that will be attractive and valuable to the business: we can consider using corporate branding on screen designs (especially important if this will be seen by customers); security will be evident but not intrusive; there will be common utilities to provide supporting document management and knowledge, information and data management capabilities; access to corporate applications will be provided on a controlled basis; and internet access will support administrative requirements (e.g. travel, car hire and probably much more). There will be local network devices for printing and the network will support voice and video as well as data. Customers and suppliers may have access, as will remote workers, and there may be collaboration tools. Data will be accessed in a managed way to support large-scale data storage and retrieval. There will be backup and recovery systems and services, email, groupware and applications. Depending upon the industry sector there may be other specific devices attached to the network (e.g. EPOS, ATM, scanning devices, GPS systems etc.). At the level of reassurance there will be a management regime to track events (monitoring, detection, logging, examination and filtering, processing, correlation, escalation, resolution, closure, lifecycle, grouping, reporting etc.). There will be operational control of the services, components and their configuration. There will be workload management, scheduling, output management, resilience testing, management of supporting processes and performance monitoring, auditing and tuning. In short, the infrastructure can either be loaded up with standard features that were previously considered to be major cost items requiring significant investment and supported by first-class management practices or it can be stripped down to deprive the business customer of everything of value in the name of corporate control. There seems to be no half measure. What kind of business infrastructure does your business have access to?

Leadership of product and service design

Products need to be designed with a view of the market in mind. They need product champions but also we need to be able to recognise the products as being from the same stable; we expect them to have the same look and feel. Product champions used by commercial services providers will be within the services organisation, with a major reseller or with the vendor itself. In businesses with internal services providers, the champions and the funding for internal product development will usually reside within the business unless the product has become universal within the business in which case 'ownership' may have transferred to the internal service provider. Leadership must exist for the requirements to be defined, investment decisions to be taken and for the products and services (and the business they support) to thrive.

Closeness here is about the business need being satisfied in terms of having the use of the most appropriate solutions for the business with new requirements being satisfied in a timely manner. This involves establishing an awareness of what is required and what will be of value to the business both now and in the future, selecting or designing relevant high-value products and services and having the agility to make choices and deliver the solutions quickly.

When there is a lack of leadership in this area, decisions become short term and shifts in the market become more problematic for the IT people to cope with. If a champion withdraws support for a product or service it will whither unless another champion is quickly found.

Product and service delivery

Having defined the requirement and designed the solution we must deliver it. This may be about delivering a new software product or solution, a business change or a service.

Most approaches reflect their origin. Within the IT community there have historically been two groups of delivery services; the first group develops and delivers solutions (development and integration), the second provides a day-to-day service (sometimes referred to as IT operations). People in each group are intensely loyal to their origin. Both groups often vie for customer attention instead of working through value-add intermediaries. In reality the business often fails to differentiate: if either the development engine or the operations engine is under-performing then the whole of IT delivery will be seen to be under-performing. This will also be true if any aspect is subcontracted or outsourced and a supplier is under-performing. For the purpose of assessment we examine each but the IT service provider must remember this joint responsibility and the customer perception.

Operations management

To many operations management is the domain of service management, ITIL and perhaps ISO/IEC 20000. Complementing and partially overlapping these is COBIT or perhaps a proprietary model from one of the hardware vendors or large service providers. These are all very useful in terms of improving our understanding of what to do or providing a 'how to' framework but again they are all very IT-focused. Unfortunately it is not helpful to inform the customer that the service (whatever it is) experience must be great because it complies with a particular approach, even where compliance may be a prerequisite to being able to supply. On a day-to-day basis it is the business experience that matters and this includes performance, outcomes and the complexities of brand.

The usefulness of a methodology such as ITIL or a standard such as ISO/IEC 20000 is that it draws every service provider's attention to the core processes of service delivery in the operations arena. If everyone adopts the same standard then it can help to establish common processes, a common language and common interfaces. ITIL is rapidly becoming the de-facto framework of choice in the operations management area. ISO/IEC 20000 is still structured according to the old ITIL framework and requires service delivery processes encompassing capacity management, service continuity and availability management, service-level management and service reporting. We have control processes for configuration management and change management. Resolution processes include incident management and problem management. Finally we have release management processes. We have not included information security, budgeting and accounting, business relationship management or supplier management because these are dealt with elsewhere and we would argue that they should not exist separately if the organisation embraces services other than operations. Within ITIL v3 this area is addressed by the service transition (transition planning, asset and configuration management, release and deployment management, change management and testing and validation) and service operation (event management, request fulfilment, incident management, problem management and access management) processes. The impact of ITIL is particularly impressive in terms of delivering successful outcomes where services organisations are at an early stage of their development (i.e. they are low on the IT maturity scale). However the more a standard is adopted the more pressure there will be on the remaining service providers in the industry to adopt the standard in order to simplify interfaces, until that is methods, needs or expectations change. An unexpected benefit that has been especially helpful is where organisations have developed release management processes for extending the functionality, reach or deployment of product or service as opposed to using generalised project management methods.

There is much to be done to standardise the terminology across the various standards and methods. It is often different and where it is necessary to adopt multiple international standards in the delivery area the overlaps could be handled better. The final concern is that the international standards framework is incomplete and we illustrated this earlier by comparing what is formalised in some way with the full scope of what we now believe to be necessary as illustrated by the ITDYNAMICS™ service engine concept.

Probably the second most widely used approach to improving the delivery organisation is through the application of COBIT. It can be used on its own or in conjunction with ITIL. COBIT has developed from an audit process to a governance process over recent years designed to balance and manage control requirements, technical issues and business risks. Once more the emphasis is on IT process (domains, processes and activities) but it broadens this to the IT resources (people, application systems, technology, facilities and data) and the information criteria (quality, fiduciary and security) needed for delivery. The three dimensions (i.e. the IT processes, IT resources and information criteria) are referred to as the COBIT cube. It cites business orientation as its main theme using critical success factors, key goal indicators and KPIs and is designed to be used at the business level to asses the health of IT. As can be seen from the dimensions of the cube it is in fact very IT-focused. Like ITIL it focuses on defining and delivering IT and contributes greatly to understanding some of the IT processes. COBIT is slightly broader in scope although it is less specific than ITIL in terms of defining the operational processes. Although it is often used by the IT service provider as a governance framework, a business manager would need an IT background to assess their IT service in this way. Work has been completed recently to identify the overlaps and to cross reference COBIT to ITIL and this is now available either from itSMF (ITIL) or from ISACA (COBIT). These may be helpful to those organisations that do try to use both frameworks but this collaboration just serves to emphasise the additional complexity and we hope that this will be addressed over the coming years. When business has asked IT to provide a way in which it can be assessed, IT has tended to respond with IT process which reflects current best (technical) practice. We have to restore the supremacy of outcome over process if best practice is to have any meaningful value. We must favour those activities that have a direct bearing on the outcome to the customer rather than those which can become secondary, technology dependent or process related. In short we must begin to think more about what we achieve in business terms rather than how we work as technical institutions.

SLAs can encapsulate desired outcomes. If these focus mainly on how well we adhere to process we may have issues because then the process has become the end rather than the means. It follows then that the choice of metrics within the SLA is important because these will directly influence behaviour. For example we all recognise the difference between the terms time to fix and time to respond. The first sets an expectation in terms of when a repair or remedy will have been completed and the second does not.

Performance criteria should be understandable, relevant, realistic, accurate, comparable and timely. Performance is normally recorded and reported if it is relevant to a SLA, a process that has a process owner or a programme or project. Other specific examples of performance measurement might apply to benchmark comparisons (a comparison with a standard or with another similar organisation), continuous improvement (a comparison with our own earlier performance and target), risk management (a comparison of events and perceived likelihood and impact), the PIR (a comparison with our delivery objectives) and the exploitation of time zones (a comparison of the time worked against the time available). We may use efficiency or productivity measures such as incidents closed (problems solved), speed or response times, orders processed, items delivered, resources used, queries answered, procedures introduced, transactions processed, users supported, software patches installed, machines upgraded etc.

Increasingly the trend is to report performance using business-focused measures so that they can be used within the business. These should have the advantages of being tangible and easily understood (e.g. incidents reported per week versus machine man-hours). This may be broken down by the type of incident to demonstrate the reliability of systems or the differences in requests for help in different departments (to highlight training needs) etc. There is merit in being creative by adding business value to statistics.

Sometimes we need to measure or assess our service using more qualitative criteria. These may be about availability of information and facilities to create competitive advantage, the extent to which a system can be personalised, process flexibility, the quality of documentation and help screens, responsiveness to change or change requests, levels of business confidence, opinions on training materials and facilities. In these cases we should use different mechanisms to focus on the key issues and then measure these key aspects differently to remove any ambiguity from the equation. For example instead of asking for opinions on training, we should have a focus group meeting to explore everyone's views concerning training. If the group decides that the key issue is that we need to increase the take-up of training because they think that this will improve performance, the next stage is to gather evidence by measuring the take-up of training materials and facilities across all products and customers and then to examine the correlation between performance and the take-up of training. If the correlation is strong we formulate a plan and test this out in different situations to see there if we can improve the take-up. We then monitor performance and if it increases we formulate a plan to increase the take-up more widely.

In the 1970s Jan Carlzon of Scandinavian Airlines fame talked about the 'moments of truth': those moments when we have an immediate opportunity to provide value to the customer (Carlzon 1989). These are often during face-to-face meetings, telephone conversations, sales situations or when the customer has a complaint. They are often characterised by the customer or business having a problem (maybe of our own making) and the service provider finding a solution to that problem. These days IT service providers typically create a single point of contact for the business to handle many such situations. This can be variously referred to as a call centre, a contact centre, a help desk or a service desk. The name we use implies the level of service that we might expect (i.e. a call centre apparently implies a lower level of service than a service desk). Most people would not recognise the significance of the name but there will always be an expectation that the service desk will fix the problem and this will be perceived to be of high business value if it all works well. These are often not just single points of contact but critical points of contact for those who use them. In some environments there may be an obligation to report a failure to an authorised body.

It is interesting to note then how many organisations provide not just an inadequate single point of contact but one where the service standards are not defined according to customer needs. The business customer simply wants a fast and certain response to the enquiry or problem. Those that service the consumer, SME and home office markets often do so at the lowest possible cost and do more harm to those services providers than they can possibly imagine. Many are unfit for purpose. The acid test is whether you would wish your most important business customer to call the service desk number if it becomes necessary for that person to do so. Whether it is the business CEO or anyone else in the organisation that is unable to proceed without help, they should get the same standard of service. In business this directly affects productivity. In the consumer market it influences repeat purchase or renewal. From a business perspective the best service desks are multi-skilled or at least appear to be so, supported by knowledge-based systems and capable of fixing 90–100% of all problems during the first call. Clearly this will depend upon the nature of the business and the resources and funding available but where problems have to be escalated to higher levels there will be logging, escalation and queue management features. There is also a need to record and track incidents and complaints to establish trends. Where problems cannot be resolved immediately it is important that customers are kept informed of request status and progress. ISO/IEC 20000 has recognised this and is a requirement of this standard.

When a call is received it is important to try to resolve the customer problem; if this is not possible it will be necessary to make an initial assessment by gathering as much information as possible to help to diagnose and fix the problem or transfer the customer immediately to the subject expert for resolution. In the worst case it will be necessary to commit to getting back within a period covered by agreed service levels (and these should be realistic from a customer perspective). If the services organisation cannot respond quickly the problem must be escalated consistent with the SLA and, in the case of suspected hardware failure, it is helpful if loan equipment can be provided whilst the problem is being fixed. The supporting systems must manage the request lifecycle including closure and verification. There should be a response to the customer as part of the verification process.

Ideally the call will be answered immediately without a menu of options. All service staff will be operating in the native language of their business customer and located in a region where the legal system offers similar protection should personal data be accessible. The service organisation will know about us, the systems we are using and it will be intimately familiar with the products it supports and service availability. The service desk staff will not prompt us to leave a message (no added value), seek to generate a lead, refer us to anyone else without good reason, persist with a script when clearly this is inappropriate and information once given will not have to be repeated.

It is not uncommon to have to confront a complex automated menu of many levels before a call to a service desk is eventually routed to someone that will be able to deal with the problem or answer the question. There is a major services provider that places all inbound calls into just one such complex call handling and call routing system. The following examples have been experienced more than once with this same service provider. After selecting the correct menu option several times through about five different menu levels we eventually received a pre-recorded message telling us that we have to call a different number. When we call the new number we eventually get to speak to someone who neither understands what we are saying nor anything about our problem. After several minutes of very unsatisfactory conversation we are mysteriously disconnected before our problem has been either diagnosed or resolved. Presumably by disconnecting the call they were able to avoid admitting that they did not know how to fix the problem. On another occasion we needed some information about an account that was affecting our ability to logon and we received three different answers to the same question over a two-day period. The third example with this same services provider was to follow our required option through the menus only to find that we rejoined at the beginning. The operational cost of this service desk is probably close to zero. The real cost will be the lost business resulting from the poor service experience.

As organisations become more dispersed the service desk can add value by informing and seeking feedback on a wide range of issues. They become an extension of account management for distributed business people and can be used to communicate planned and short-term changes of service level to the business etc. In the consumer context service providers must recognise that outbound calling is often seen as sales-focused and callers should be prepared for a robust response if the value of the call is not immediately apparent. Outbound calls to business customers, just like calls to consumers, should not be undertaken without good market research. If the call is likely to be relevant and the caller seeks to qualify the level of interest then it can work well. This is a classic area where our experience as consumers overflows into the business environment. Outbound calling using centres in other countries can be even more problematic as they may operate in a different legislative framework to our own business and at the moment calls cannot be barred according to their country of origin.

The internal information systems must provide useful management information and recommendations for service improvement. There is high value to be obtained by the service provider by tracking the history of problems and failures. By analysing trends the astute service provider can diagnose the need for intervention strategies with either the business (e.g. by providing additional training at low cost to the people having the most difficulty) or with a third-party supplier of hardware or software where the service provider may offer to work with the supplier to improve either the functionality or the reliability of the product.

Configuration management is the means by which we provide traceability in terms of the make-up of infrastructure items. This requires discipline to identify, record and report the appropriate items, their status and the relationships between them. They are held in a configuration management database (CMDB) or configuration management system (CMS). A configuration baseline is the make-up of a product in terms of items and structures at a point in time. The CMDB or CMS provides a basis for product recall in the event of adverse performance trends, recording installed infrastructure, managing software licenses or document libraries etc.

During a call to the service desk it may become apparent that the customer requires a change to the product, service or the SLA. This needs to be managed and the process is often referred to as the request for change process. This involves identifying the requirement, the areas of impact on business and IT and the prioritisation and authorisation process. The configuration database must be updated and the schedule associated with the change must be communicated; the release management process must be transparent in the sense that priority, status and progress should be visible.

So what kind of reporting helps us to manage these activities? We must have the statistics to undertake site or customer analysis and trending. As a customer business we must have similar information: we must know how well each location is supported and how well each supplier is performing. There is more about this under the heading of supplier management.

The customer satisfaction survey is worthy of consideration immediately following the call to the service desk. These limited-focus direct-feedback mechanisms are the best use of the survey technique as they are related to a specific event. These should happen routinely after every call, be communicated over the internet or intranet, be very short and collect qualitative as well as quantitative data. Never assume that a nil return is an indication of satisfaction: it is more likely to be the opposite. Customers exasperated by the service desk response to calls for help are unlikely to bother to answer a questionnaire. This is why such surveys can appear to conflict with anecdotal evidence. There may be a case for other regular evaluation mechanisms such as the 'mystery shopper' or focus groups but the questions that need to be asked in focus groups will develop as the service and technology changes; this means that comparative results collected over an extended period of time are often meaningless. Owing to the limited scope everything other than the direct feedback mechanisms specific to a call needs to become part of the assessment of the total business experience.

Regardless of the approach taken to managing service delivery and the service desk, the service provider will have complaints. There should be documented policies and procedures to define how to deal with complaints so that they are recorded and managed. The policy should provide for a response to all complainants and incidents should be monitored and trends assessed and reported. For complaints to be a useful source of management information they should be handled independently of the service desk function.

Programme and project management

When the service provider is delivering a solution or change it has to think about what others think it is delivering. It must consider business expectations (desired outcomes) and then think about how it will meet them (processes). Service providers will have to decide whether the approach is one of programme management or project management. We usually talk about these techniques as though they are totally different or maybe that programmes are bigger and more complex than projects (e.g. multiple projects).

Programmes can have complexities that projects do not: budgets tend to be bigger, they are often dealing with business change, there may be parallel workstreams with interdependencies, milestones will not easily be established, there will be many uncertainties, there will be a need to have access to a 'senior responsible owner' and there will be a responsibility to contribute towards business benefits realisation. In fact this could also describe many things we call projects.

Perhaps the most useful differentiator is that programme management more usually implies not just taking responsibility for the IT outcome but also leading the business change. The change may be IT driven, it might be about leading a business transition following some kind of acquisition or merger or it might be about taking responsibility for an aspect of the business plan involving major market growth or business turnaround. In all of these situations the programme manager is taking responsibility for aspects of business leadership, management process (the means), financial management, relationship management, resource management, project management, task order management, supplies management and services management. There is a constant need to balance short-term challenges with long-term objectives. There is a need to maintain a strategic focus whilst delivering short-term gains. Programmes must be aligned with business and marketing objectives.

Change management has always been a high-risk activity. The number of unexpected problems that can arise during the life of a major IT-driven business change programme can be awesome. A few of the more obvious examples are:

- hardware not ready;
- software not ready;

- poor business change or leadership skills;
- testing is incomplete;
- telecommunications problems;
- skills shortage;
- forced personnel changes (sickness, leavers etc.);
- unforeseen cost increases;
- inability to get total business commitment;
- consultation over redundancies caused by the business change;
- inability to define requirement;
- late delivery of a critical resource;
- poor internal and external communication;
- data, security or privacy exposures;
- poor project management;
- training needs not identified;
- late changes to the business requirement;
- funding issues;
- unstable business trading environment;
- poor strategy or planning leading to need for clarification.

These risks cannot be eliminated completely by using a methodology; any methodology that has to handle every eventuality would be too complex to use. The risks can however be reduced by appointing a highly competent independent programme manager who will take control of the programme and adopt a business-focused approach.

Programme management is a means of managing many resources and many variables in order to deliver a desired outcome to the business. Successful programme managers both manage and recover major change programmes. What differentiates a good programme manager from an average one is experience. Experienced programme managers have frequently had to succeed where others have failed and if we distil the reasons for this success we see an extreme business-focused skill set. These business-focused programme management techniques can be formalised and incorporated into the way we manage programmes in order to reduce business risk and increase business value. There is a lot of good material available on programme and project management but as the failure rate of IT-driven change programmes is so high it is worth elaborating on the fundamental importance of how we approach, manage and govern programmes.

Many approaches to programme management concentrate on the fact that a programme consists of multiple projects: get the project delivery right and the programme will progress satisfactorily. Sadly this is often not the case and if we are over-burdened with governance arrangements, such as where there are project boards as well as a programme board, it is very difficult for a business to drive through the necessary programme priorities; an individual project board can exert undue influence on the whole programme. It is important to ensure that whatever project management methods are used they can accommodate new techniques (e.g. the recent changes in delivery methods using extreme or agile methods). We need to adapt our management methods to address the ever-changing needs using a wider range of controls than has been common in IT. A business-focused approach to programme management is a more relevant and appropriate business-driven approach to change management that:

- has different dynamics;
- has a different emphasis;
- is more responsive in delivery to the needs of the business.

The dynamics of business-focused programme management. The experienced programme manager's approach is illustrated in Figure 3.16.

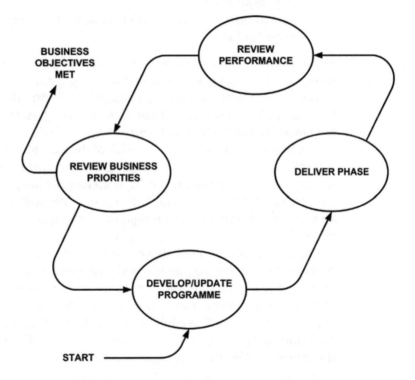

FIGURE 3.16 *Approach to programme management*

The problem with many large programmes is that the business need is changing constantly and service delivery organisations fail to respond appropriately. The approach of the experienced programme manager is to expect change and to work very closely with the business in order to assess the impact on the programme. The programme will develop around the priorities of the business, adopting a phased approach focused on delivering early successes. A phase is typically a 90-day time period and can consist of many interdependent projects, part projects or tasks. At the conclusion of each phase we review progress and business priorities and then update the programme plan and investment portfolio.

In this way we are always delivering value and the programme is always in step with the business. Furthermore, the programme ends when the business has achieved its goals, not when all of the planned projects are complete. In short, the dynamics ensure that more value is delivered at less risk.

It sounds simple but to manage a programme in this way the programme manager must be able to manage:

- downwards, in terms of the delivery aspects of projects and tasks;
- upwards, in terms of the business alignment aspects of priorities, phases and value;
- side to side, in terms of suppliers and other external stakeholder organisations.

As former IT project managers most programme managers are able to deal with managing downwards with a greater or lesser degree of competence. Fewer are equipped through both experience and training to deal with managing upwards. Many programme managers are employed by the prime contractor or supplier and so are unable to act wholly in the business interest in terms of the side-to-side management.

Ideally a change programme should be managed by the business but few business people have the skills to manage a change programme that has any significant IT content. This again emphasises the importance of an experienced independent programme manager working on behalf of the business.

The approach described above is a form of continuous improvement process applied to programme delivery; there is a constant readjustment and realignment of the plan as we learn more about the changing business requirement. This can be continued into development by the appropriate choice of development tools to accelerate solution delivery. Anything approaching real-time business change will also reduce many of the gaps identified in the service excellence model.

The emphasis of business-focused programme management. The emphasis in project-oriented methods is, not surprisingly, the project. To minimise risk and to achieve better alignment with the business we have to change the emphasis to the over-arching programme, as illustrated in Figure 3.17.

The vast majority of the resources used to deliver a change programme are deployed at the project level. It is easy to see then that if projects are

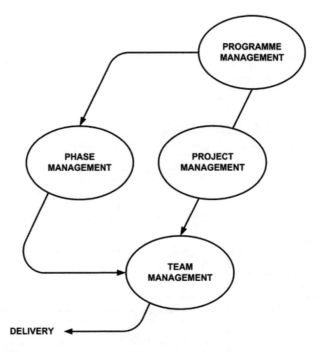

FIGURE 3.17 *Phase management in controlling team resource*

not aligned with the business (and programme) that things can get out of control.

The programme board must represent all key stakeholders and must have total control over the decisions regarding the phasing of the programme, the prioritisation of tasks and the deployment of resources to tasks. By introducing the concept of the phase, directed by the programme manager and the business, it is possible to control the velocity (delivered business value and direction of delivery). Only in this way can value be delivered in line with the changing needs and priorities of the business.

Responsiveness of business-focused programme management. A typical high-level programme plan is illustrated in Figure 3.18. It will be supported by a more detailed Gantt chart with dependencies and resourcing plans.

Time is shown on the horizontal axis, the horizontal bars represent projects and phases are the vertical 90-day divisions of time. Clearly this can only represent the plan at a point in time because the dynamics and the emphasis explained above allow us to change the plan and the resource allocation according to the changing needs of the business.

This approach can also help a business to get a change programme under control that may be late or over budget. Re-establishing control over the deployment of project resources to better reflect business priorities can be a dramatic first step to recovering a runaway program.

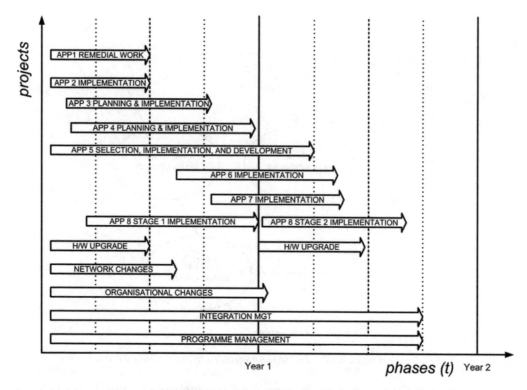

FIGURE **3.18**   *A phased program*

The net effect is again a more relevant and appropriate business-driven approach to change management that is increasingly in demand within both the private and public sector. The consequence of adopting this approach is a classic programme plan of project and phase but it is more dynamic and responsive to the business need. By adopting it at the outset the success rate of major change programmes can increase dramatically.

The approach can encapsulate any other methodology. For example organisations may recognise that this approach goes beyond the project-oriented philosophy of their chosen methodology and yet still makes their programmes business-focused without wasting their investment in training. Improved planning and control techniques from Burke (1999) or others should also be introduced to increase project success rates.

Business-focused project management. Project management methods work best where there are a group of tasks that can be defined and estimated and managed to their conclusion. PRINCE2 is probably the best known project management method in the UK but there are others advocated by the American Project Management Institute (PMI) and there are the ISEB Certificates in IS Project Management (see Hughes et al. (2004)) which have additional worthwhile content describing 'how to' whereas PRINCE2 defines 'what', 'when' and 'by whom'. 'Business-focused IT' techniques can be used with all of these.

These methods present a huge body of knowledge and can provide a framework that will be based on industry best practice for project planning and initiation, directing and controlling a project or project stage, managing a stage boundary, managing product delivery and project close. They will help to plan, define the components, the business case, project organisation, controls, risk management, project quality, configuration management and change management. We need to be able to derive work breakdown structures, workflow, risk and issues logs and a structure for quality reviews. Finally the project methods help by being prescriptive about the types of roles that are required (e.g. chairperson, producer, reviewers, scribe, project manager, team manager, project assurance roles and project support roles). The weakness of creating all of these roles and tasks is that we will have to satisfy these requirements thus adding to the workload. We have to be careful that we are not inadvertently creating unnecessary work.

At worst a methodology based on massive bodies of knowledge can induce massive and unnecessary administrative overhead to fulfil a purpose that is tangential to the purpose of the project rather than central to the project. The characteristic of over-burdensome methodologies is the 'project template': intentionally or unintentionally, as methods mature there are organisations that offer predefined activities designed to comply with the requirements of the customer that specifies compliance with that method. This is particularly attractive to immature buying or supply organisations. It is not unusual to come across complex project Gantt charts populated with some 400 activities, none of which actually add any value or contribute to delivering anything at all. Far from reducing risk these almost guarantee failure. Ironically the motive is often to reduce risk by using a methodology with the expectation that this will bring project success. A common cause of failure is where project management methods are being applied inappropriately to more complex problems that would be better treated using the programme management techniques described earlier. The problem these organisations have is that they do not have anyone with the necessary skills to manage a programme so they manage it as a project and assume that a methodology will handle the complexities. There is no substitute for experience: basic management ability and an over-prescribed project template is no substitute for a good programme manager.

Let us just consider the basics of project management. The why, what, how, who and when of project management defines the business context, the business objectives (targets), the scope and structure of the approach, the resources needed, when we start, how we schedule the tasks, the project dependencies and the project timescales. The work breakdown structure shows the estimates of the work involved, the logical dependencies and how responsibilities are to be assigned.

Then there is risk management. We must assess the likely impact on the project and likelihood of each perceived risk.

We must decide how much slack should be allowed for slippages. We often over-estimate the margin. We need to base delivery dates on a thorough understanding of contributing parties and yet few of us have confidence in the estimates of others, even when tied into tight contracts. Time and cost management are important skills but few have the right experience or success rate. Goldratt (1997) proposes ways in which to deal with this issue in his works on the theory of constraints and the critical chain theory of project management.

Frequent problems are as follows: issue reporting and tracking is often poor; we fail to accept the reality of the situation; we fail to adequately manage change; we fail to separate factors external to the change from the metrics we are collecting about the change itself; we fail to deal with resources (in this case people) by not assigning clear roles and responsibilities; and so on. All of this means that it is usually very difficult to sensibly report progress against plan or budget or timescales. The metrics we apply must go beyond the simple metrics of progress.

If we invest in a project office we must make sure that it is producing useful information. If we cannot afford the overhead then we must make sure that the tasks, their outcomes and the measures of progress are well defined and then get the project manager to report on a regular basis. We must also pick managers that will not hide bad news until it is too late.

Sometimes a service provider will enter into a fixed price contract. These contractual arrangements are often required in order to submit a compliant bid. Not all organisations have the ability to estimate accurately or manage effectively to be sure of meeting a fixed price. In essence these service providers simply accept the risk and hope it works out. They are playing the odds. This is why large organisations prefer to deal with large suppliers; if they fail they are big enough to accept the consequences. The large service providers in turn will hope to leave enough loopholes in their contracts to enable them to absolve themselves of any financial liability for late delivery. There is however an alternative approach. If large businesses were to employ experienced independent managers to manage projects and service providers the risks could be drastically reduced.

We all learn from experience but how many people actually learn from the PIR? The PIR is the process intended for us all to learn where we could have done better and so improve the process for the next time. Sadly the PIR is often a formality; worse still it is often a process for apportioning blame or dealing with criticism. There are two reasons for undertaking a PIR: where the service provider wishes to understand what went well and where the process needs to be improved in the future, or where the business wishes to be sure that the benefits ascribed to the solution when the project was sanctioned have actually been achieved. Most IT service delivery organisations will undertake some kind of PIR. Fewer businesses will be motivated to undertake a PIR unless there has been some kind of major delivery failure. It is not that they have no interest but rather that businesses are already onto the next project and cannot spare valuable or scarce resource to look back at a process that was probably considered to be satisfactory. The service provider should then focus on its own processes and ensure that the business acknowledges that the solution was delivered professionally and meets all objectives.

Approach to programme recovery. Some of us have the pleasure of bringing wayward change programmes back to plan. If we approach this with a mindset that a methodology has not been followed then we are probably on the wrong track. You may have guessed from the discussion so far that actually the methodology is not always terribly relevant. What may be relevant is how a methodology may have blinded us into thinking that risks were being managed when in fact they were simplifying the issues such that they were missed and not managed.

It is a fact that when tasked with recovering a wayward programme the first things to be sacrificed are any inappropriate governance mechanisms. It is important to gain control of the resources and have open communications with all key stakeholders: mechanisms that facilitate this are OK but those that do not are not.

Having gained control of the resources we can start to take decisions about the variables. We must determine:

- where we are now;
- where we want to get to;
- what is required;
- what can be delivered;
- what we are prepared to spend;
- what the best solution is given the situation we are in;
- which of the major stakeholders will support the proposed recovery strategy.

Once we have the answers to these questions we must establish a detailed work breakdown structure, develop a revised resourcing plan, calculate what the work will cost and when it will be completed and then drive it forward. We must remember to keep in touch with the key stakeholders on a regular basis to keep them informed of progress and to find out what is happening to the business requirement, the trading environment and business priorities. If recovery is approached in this way it is not unusual for as much as 40% of the original requirement to 'evaporate' as we re-establish the key drivers of the project.

Software development. We have already mentioned the emergence of agile methods. These will evolve as speed to market, cost and quality become more important and as new business-focused tools become available. Tapscott and Williams (2007) describe how IBM adapted to working with open source developers. They had to reject the traditional waterfall approach to spend more time on implementation, testing and support. They had to embrace collaborative development practices using instantaneous back-and-forth communications using email and instant messaging to achieve rapid product iterations. This combined with the latest business process and service-oriented architectures will soon change the application landscape. We will have continuous improvement processes for rapid solution development that will enable us to create unique solutions for competitive advantage that will be as feature rich as some of today's packages or packages that can be enhanced easily without the normal development costs and support implications we associate with customisation.

Application management. An important aspect of service from the IT service provider may be the management of key applications, particularly if these represent a major investment for the business and are perceived to provide competitive advantage.

The service provider will need to obtain approval for a maintenance contract or agreement that defines what level of support, maintenance and development is required in order that the appropriate skills and resources can be allocated. There will be an agreed plan for future releases of the application.

The business will want to know who is responsible for managing each major application or group of applications. The business will expect documented procedures, development proposals and plans to ensure that the business retains its competitiveness and in order that it may protect its investment. It will expect some kind of report that clearly sets out how the product is performing against some clear performance criteria in such a way that trends can be identified. It may have SLAs in which case the product reports will be described in relation to those SLAs. If there is a development project in train it will expect to receive a progress report that compares progress against the project plan and how the emerging product compares with the design objectives. Perhaps the key performance criteria include speed or response times, accessibility, access to external data, the extent to which the system can be personalised, flexibility, the quality of documentation, help facilities, usage etc. Risk management will be important to the business as will user confidence. On the other hand the business will be wanting information to enable it to judge the capability of the delivery organisation, such as actual productivity versus productivity targets, performance versus benchmark comparisons, how adequately the service provider is meeting any performance targets that have been agreed, how adequately the service provider is meeting the configuration management requirements, how competent the service provider is at business change, how responsive the service provider is to change or change requests etc. What about release management, security management, capacity management, incident management, problem management, availability management, service continuity management, service level management, resource and manpower management, financial management, user training and business continuity plans?

Release management. Where a supplier of product or service regularly releases a largely standard product or service to new communities there is little point in creating a new project each time. There will be a need for a rudimentary project framework in order to measure progress and success but the process is routinely repeated and so both customers and suppliers would be better served by having a well-tried and well-proven release management system. Once proven these work like clockwork and represent almost zero risk. In short whenever this can be achieved there will be a reduction in terms of resource, cost and risk. What we are doing is switching from integration or project thinking to service management thinking and in the process saving effort and cost.

Quality management

Quality management and quality systems are important in terms of achieving consistency in terms of product quality, service performance and service improvement.

Problematically all aspects of management concerned with these goals are often grouped under this heading instead of being a line management responsibility. Services also vary. Some are very conducive to highly developed service or quality procedures that can guarantee high performance on every occasion. Others frankly are more creative and depend upon the skills and insight of a particular analyst and a spark between that person and the business manager: in this situation the track record is what will sell the service. As when 'crossing the chasm' (Moore 1991) the need to address market-oriented issues as well as technical ones can apply here also.

Our reasons for investing in quality management can vary. We may be seeking to introduce fundamental changes arising from some business process reengineering activity or we may have aspirations of business or service excellence; either of these we would consider to be 'Big Q' challenges. Alternatively we may be looking to introduce process documentation, minor incremental improvements to a process or we may simply be aiming for certification or accreditation in order to prequalify to supply a prospective customer. This may be a step along the way to establishing a more disciplined organisation; the organisation may be steeped in the ways of quality improvement or it may wish to simply put a tick in the box by introducing a documented, formal and accredited quality management system. These we could consider as 'Little Q'.

In fact many Little Q organisations think that most of the benefits can be achieved by simply aiming for compliance with a particular standard rather than full accreditation. For some this cherry-picking approach with no commitment to the full process and the corresponding overhead cost can be a good solution if a tick in the box is all that is required. If the business is not motivated towards Big Q possibilities this may be a perfectly satisfactory situation.

There is clearly a connection between service excellence (mentioned earlier) and Big Q. The ITDYNAMICS™ service excellence model examines the relationship between the IT service and the business need. This leads to greater business impact (Big Q) than former methods which either consider IT for its own sake or consider an organisation's progress in terms of developing process, for example:

- the EFQM model;
- the five-point maturity scale of product orientation, process orientation, system orientation, chain orientation and total quality;
- the capability maturity model (Weber et al. 1991);
- the theory of organisational data processing growth by Gibson and Nolan (1974) which relates the phases of process maturity to DP activities.

Whilst all of these encourage us to find ways in which we can introduce improvement and to measure that improvement, some of them can move us away from business need and business outcomes and may instead encourage us to focus on Little Q. Further back in history we would argue that the quality movement when it started was much more about Big Q. The original W. Edwards Deming model describing the feedback framework (plan-do-check-action) was designed for introducing and monitoring business change. Then there is Deming's 14 point plan for a quality organisation (of which there are a number of versions) in which he suggested that we:

- plan for the long term;
- maintain an intense focus on the internal and external customer;
- show no complacency with respect to the quality of the product;
- maintain a concern for continual improvement, deal with the fewest number of suppliers;
- have statistical control over our own and our suppliers' production processes;
- develop thorough problem determination processes;
- undertake staff training that is relevant to their jobs;
- introduce and maintain a high quality of supervision;

- remove fear from the management relationship;
- encourage departments to work closely together rather than in functional silos;
- do not adhere simply to numerical goals (zero defects);
- emphasise the need for quality work, staff trained to understand statistical method;
- train staff consider how to meet new and emerging needs; and
- empower management to implement quality principles.

None of Deming's work should be considered to be Little Q. Six Sigma on the other hand may at first appear to be Little Q in as much as it is incremental in nature but such very low tolerances it frequently leads to radical decisions.

Six Sigma is designed to reduce process variation using statistical process control methods. It is based on the idea that an acceptable error rate is 3.4 defects per million opportunities. It was developed in a manufacturing environment although it has been applied to service processes with some success. The occurrences of errors on service quality must be addressed through interventions with the service provider. The intervention may involve collaboration with a supplier to bring their error rates to within agreed levels and so reduce the cost of quality to the business. Experience has shown that the costs of quality related activities fall dramatically as quality increases, for example it is estimated that for a two sigma organisation the cost of quality is approximately 50% of sales (i.e. is spent on non-value-add activities), at three to four sigma (where most organisations operate) the cost of non-value-add activities is around 15–25% and at the six sigma level the cost of quality drops to 1–2% of sales. Six Sigma as a management discipline has been used to great effect most notably by GE but also by others, often in conjunction with other performance improving techniques. The cost of quality is an interesting metric that is worth investigating. It is particularly important to monitor this alongside other controls during times of business growth or business downsizing in order to ensure that the costs stay within reasonable bounds.

Also part of Big Q is the way we measure major change programmes. We have to measure each project or task: we must measure progress against plan and establish measures of success so that we know that we are happy with the quality of what is being achieved. As well as monitoring the individual components we have to monitor the whole programme for progress and success against plan but also against objectives and make sure we have control of the resources and can influence the stakeholders. By applying methodology to this we often inadvertently treat it as Little Q.

Little Q is the domain of the quality standards, quality procedures and methodologies, many of which are a prerequisite for major supply contracts. International standards provide us with a view of industry best practice driven by 'industry consensus' and approved by at least 75% of the national bodies casting a vote. Methodologies can be pre-scribed by government agencies and again express industry best practice and are again usually driven by industry consensus. There are a number of problems with this. The first is the time it takes for expert opinion to form and for consensus to be achieved. The second is that many people in the service industry that draft or certify Little Q procedures for their clients often fail to recognise Big Q opportunities. Little Q is based on formalising process and is reinforced by those who believe that continuous incremental improvement alone will ultimately lead to business excellence. This might be the case if it was not for the fact that from time to time things fundamentally change calling for a total rethink as opposed to incremental thinking. The question for the business is deciding where the value resides. Big Q drives change; Little Q can work against it. Big Q is for innovative organisations; Little Q is for large-volume, low-risk and stable environ-ments where prescribed method is preferred and where a little tweaking is thought to be required. This is not to denigrate the approach: a little tweaking on a process that is utilised several thousand times a day can yield large savings but we do not think Little Q is what Deming, Juran and Crosby had in mind in the early days of the quality movement.

Organisations that are sincere about quality and quality improvement will explore all manner of ways in which major process improvement can be achieved but a large investment in quality procedures can inhibit change because radical change can be just too difficult to implement. Furthermore a large investment in quality management policies, quality management processes and procedures, records and change procedures can add cost and reduce agility without achieving anything of value. In building a quality management system someone has to analyse and formalise what the organisation does and herein often lies the missed opportunity. Instead of grasping this as an opportunity to review and improve core process and eliminate waste, many quality management analysts will happily document what is done today without challenging what is being formalised. Moreover most of what is drafted in these circumstances is written to obtain certification or accreditation: it becomes a quality management system describing process that has little relevance to the business of the organisation, little to do with the process of adding value and just an overhead. Once a quality management system is in place we have to demonstrate that it is being used and so it becomes a constant additional cost to the business. A process that adds no value but was thought incorrectly to be required by the buying organisation is detrimen-tal to all of the principles of the quality movement and yet we see these kinds of processes in the quality management systems of many businesses. This is not a rant about quality procedures but a plea for organisations to develop them in a way that helps organisations to introduce improvement.

What characterises the product or service delivery arena is maturity. Maturity breeds methods and standards. We see an enormous body of knowledge in this area and used correctly it is a great resource. It also enables inexperienced people to feel confident that they can manage major programmes yet when we looked at the effectiveness of project and change management over the last 20 or more years we found that there has been little or no improvement in delivered performance. Also this is an area that is undergoing change and standards built around a former way of doing things could actually conspire to inhibit the changes that are taking place. What can we do to improve things in this critical area of delivery? It is interesting to observe the ways in which this manifests itself. There seems to be a cycle of emphasis between the real and the surreal, from outcome to process, and back. Regardless of which aspect of service we consider maturity brings method, methods bring standards, standards bring process and a focus on process can lead us to forget outcomes. Perhaps it is healthier to talk about approach and not methodology? Methodologies are very prescriptive to ensure that every one undertakes tasks in the same way; the focus is on process and for some organisations this is important. What is important for 'business-focused IT' is that we approach the most critical activities in a consistently effective way, the focus being on outcome. Master practitioners do not slavishly follow methodologies but will adopt effective approaches and will select the methods they need according to the tasks to be undertaken.

We should choose our standards carefully and formalise processes only when we are happy that they are optimised for the market, the circumstances and the technology that we are dealing with. We should keep them under review so that they do not become a burden: even the most optimal processes can become obsolete without us changing them as the world changes around us. Targets must also be regularly reviewed and revised. This is continuous improvement (or as ITIL v3 calls it 'continual improvement'). Hammer (1996) talks about the need for incremental redesign and radical redesign: or total quality management and reengineering. Hammer says that organisations reach a point where there is a need to replace process as opposed to modifying process and that this is reached by identifying performance gaps. That was in 1996. By 2000 Ridderstråle and Nordström were saying that IT will mean the death of the intermediary, that IT perfects markets and that we are back in the bazaar, although this time in cyberspace (Ridderstråle and Nordström 2002). They say that organisations with lousy 'infostructures' will look like '65-year olds competing in the Olympic marathon wearing high heels and evening gowns'. This is hardly the stuff of incremental improvement. They challenge the major institutions to become creative, innovative or entrepreneurial in order to survive. The dynamics of demand and supply framework under these circumstances becomes a strategy for survival; we are being confronted by change where things are just different and we need to approach things from a different perspective. Ridderstråle and Nordström say we should approach things instead from the customer or business perspective. They talk about building the emotional enterprise and they are critical of the ways in which organisations have managed quality over the last 20 years. Put another way, Little Q can subsume Big Q. Little Q is probably an accidental by-product of our attempts to institutionalise Big Q. The Juran's quality spiral was always about Big Q (Juran and Gryna 1993). The quality spiral was a continuous improvement process of moving customer requirements, product development, operational excellence and marketing to ever-higher levels. Deming and Juran established the basis for the Kaizen (incremental change) instinct which in the west became institutionalised as quality procedures and standards and to many the original meaning of Kaizen has been lost.

Procedures and standards without Kaizen can become an expensive overhead. Perhaps some people have seen that they can derive power by imposing and measuring something other than outcome. Some methodologies have evolved into publishing tasks of mammoth proportions. The established methodologies frequently address multiple objectives. They were originally developed to produce the outputs that we would expect from an IT assignment. However some have become a process that tries to enable large service providers to work in the same way across the globe and to try to enable people who are relatively new to IT to successfully undertake large and complex assignments. The consequences of this are that even small and straightforward projects can become large and complex with no guarantee of success. Once a method is in place the standards follow. Unfortunately this has another negative influence: as process and standards are developed on method or methodology, it can take time for these standards to be put in place and when the technologies (and the methods) change we still have the standard. Thus the standard is always behind the curve. This explains why most standards are less effective than we might at first expect. Where people are relatively inexperienced, any kind of guide or library of material is useful, but one has to ask the question that, for the important projects at least, would it not be better to employ people who know what they are doing?

We must rely less on method and more on 'closeness', more on experience and more on outcomes and we should expect improvement. We should plan more effectively: establishing what has to be done, correctly assessing the risks, identifying dependencies and knowing how we will know when we have finished. We must bring as much experience and informed opinion as possible to bear on the problem and use techniques such as the Delphi method rather more. We must change our view of the scope of what we are tackling, not just delivering a project or change but providing a positive experience to the business and delivering value. Every business transaction now touches IT and we have every opportunity to be seen to excel; we must grasp these opportunities and not be too quick to stifle them with standards. Finally we must demand better international standards.

Leadership in product and service delivery

Ask a business manager what they think about leadership in this area and they will say that they expect the services provider to deliver what it promises. Separating solutions and services only makes sense to the service provider, not to the business. So businesses will look for leadership in terms of consistent delivery performance across the range of products and services. Where a major change programme is taking place in the business the programme manager will need access to senior stakeholders at boardroom level and the board will need to have visibility of the change programme. Internally the service provider will look for leadership in each product or service line and must have someone who can present a coherent picture of all products and services supplied to a business. Sometimes this is the CIO; sometimes it is an account manager with responsibility for the line of business. A worrying trend has emerged recently where the different disciplines within delivery have appointed their own account managers; now how daft is that?

'Closeness to the business' in this context means delivering what is expected, in the right combination of product and service, meeting time, cost and quality standards of performance, and responding quickly to changes to the business requirement. The trend will be toward more automation of the delivery processes leaving business change as the major task and not the development, integration and service delivery.

Bought-in products and services

> Not so very long ago a supplier had a bad experience when bidding to an internal IT services provider via the organisation's purchasing division. The background research had been done, the business wanted the supply organisation to bid, the proposition suited the buying organisation and the supplier had a great track record in the sector. After spending weeks preparing and submitting several proposals at different stages of the bid process, the supplier discovered that the purchasing manager was on long-term sick leave and the person evaluating the bids was a young and very inexperienced purchasing assistant who probably did not know much at all about the business requirement, the supply industry or the intellectual content of the proposals. Needless to say the best bid was not selected. We suspect that the business is now suffering as a consequence and blaming the internal IT services provider. The supplier that failed to win the bid certainly suffered because the bidding process was costly and there was no business at the end of it.

Few IT services organisations provide their services without being dependent upon other service providers and hardware and software vendors. Selecting, managing and working with suppliers of bought-in products and services then becomes a key activity and not one to be trusted to inexperienced people. Earlier we pointed out how an appropriate supply strategy would stimulate innovation. Let us now look at this again and consider a situation where there are multiple suppliers and how this can stimulate agility.

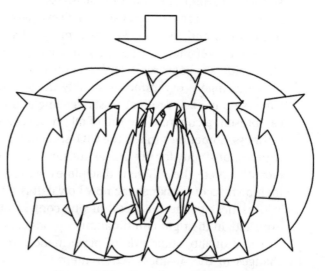

FIGURE 3.19   *Complex supply dynamics*

Instead of one supplier we now have a number, each providing access to the right skills at the right time. Accessing the market in this way reduces learning curves, creates more potentially viable solutions (choice), shortens delivery timescales, improves quality and reduces business and technical risk. Complex supply dynamics (see Figure 3.19) can be a challenge to manage but the rewards can be significant. We have been able to bring about positive remedial help to businesses by introducing greater competition into supply-side dynamics as well as time, cost and quality benefits. The IT supplier strategy needs to be managed. Over time there will be a natural churn in terms of the suppliers that the business or primary service provider chooses to work with. Technology means that we are no longer constrained by the skills of the people that we employ, only by our awareness of which organisations or people globally are best able to help us to move the business forward. Once the engagement is complete or requires different skills the supplier can be released. This flexibility combined with the ability to create endless new and innovative ideas from industry specialists is what we mean by agility.

Although every supplier wants a long-term relationship, all too often these are maintained for too long. As a consequence there may be insufficient competition to stimulate creativity and innovation. Earlier we said that creativity and innovation are at their greatest where the demand and supply cycles overlap (i.e. where the specialist supplier is responding to a business need). Some sales organisations exploit this creativity and innovation zone as a means of building the long-term relationship because they know that through consultative selling techniques they can solve customer problems, add business value and so build long-term relationships. Daffy (1999) advocates delivering customer service that will create customers for life. From a service provider's perspective these are worthy aspirations but long-term relationships do not always serve both parties well. Long-term relationships can actually inhibit flexibility because complacency can creep into the relationship. A long-term relationship may well develop but this should be based upon successive successful cycles of responding to business requirement, successful delivery and the review and revision (and realignment) of strategy by both parties. Peters (2003) described his views of the new business order and amongst the many aspects of change he discusses is how IT investment will free up a business from its bricks and mortar. He discusses how IT investment allows more opportunity for partnering and collaboration and the benefits that this can bring compared with long-term 'strategic' supplier relationships. Peters says that 'strategic suppliers have a principal goal in life relative to you (the business)…sucking up'. He goes on to say 'dull suppliers = dull you' and 'cool suppliers = cool you'. We say 'right suppliers at the right time = better business'.

> The author was managing an IT department as an interim manager. His task was to assess the internal IT organisation, develop and deliver a performance improvement programme and then recruit a full-time replacement head of IT. He recalls that the department looked to have some unexpectedly high running costs. It transpired that although the IT had largely been outsourced some years previously, the outsourced service provider had subcontracted the desktop support to another organisation but had retained some of the responsibility. It became clear that there was a significant degree of overlap between what the two companies were doing. Worse still the IT department had not fully downsized when these activities had originally been outsourced and so the business was paying for the same activity to be carried out three times by different organisations. An extreme example perhaps but a saving which more than paid for the author's fees once the problem had been discovered.

Most bought-in products and services are evaluated on the basis of their fit to the business requirement (in theory). The business makes a statement of its requirements, invites bids and ranks the proposals according to some well-considered criteria. Further down the line they assess performance against whatever product specification or SLAs they have in place. The problem with this is that the criteria we used to select the supplier may not be the same as those we use to later assess their performance. There are numerous reasons for this but the root of the problem is that things change. We need a more comprehensive way of assessing bought in services or our own management of the buying processes.

Supplier assessment or assessment of supply management

When we complete the assessment of bought-in products and services we can use it to represent different things and we have to make a choice as to which representation we will use. The most common assessment is based on how well the services provider manages its suppliers. Inevitably this often reflects the performance of the suppliers but we have just one score. Alternatively just as we propose we assess the performance of the primary service provider by considering the ten different groups of skills that contribute to the total business experience, we would suggest that this is also a great way of looking at each supplier to the service provider in some detail and of comparing multiple suppliers. The score we use for the service provider under this heading in this latter case will be the arithmetic mean of the total business experience of the suppliers it manages. To derive the arithmetic mean work out the total business experience score for each supplier, sum them and divide this by the number of suppliers.

Regardless of which of the assessments we wish to make the following points will help those tasked with undertaking the assessment.

Business and sector awareness. We have to be clear what we wish to know in this assessment. There are three possibilities: how well do they know their own specialisms, how well do they understand the business of the IT services provider and how well do they understand the business? In general we would suggest that we would be assessing the first of these because that is why they have been retained but that may not be the purpose of the assessment to be undertaken. If there is a need for the supplier to be briefed on either the business or the work of the primary service provider then arrangements must be made to extend any corporate communications programme to these suppliers or subcontractors.

Marketing and communications. We will have a view of the extent to which their marketing is consistent with that of the primary service provider. Are they delivering what they said they would deliver? Are they the business they said they were when they were selling to the service provider? Are they able to deliver what they said they would deliver? How good are they at communicating their capabilities? Do they have the same contextual view of the requirement as the service provider? And so on.

Sales and value-add. How do we feel about the supplier's sales process? Was this a process of understanding the requirement and working up a proposition that added value to the business, did they just respond to a tender or was there a feeling of indifference or even coercion? How much opportunity was there for the supplier to add value to the service provider's proposition and hence to the business? Was the opportunity used successfully? Is a commercial relationship developing or was it a single and impersonal transaction? After the contract was established was there any apparent 'deal drift' that meant that the business lost out in some way?

Sometimes the parties involved can get cold feet in the later stages of a contract being put into place. This is most common where the benefits have become less clear and in situations where there is little trust between the two parties. If this is happening then the service provider has probably not worked with that supplier before and the business should be concerned.

> We recently discovered that a large systems integrator had engaged a consultancy business to undertake the business analysis work associated with a major long-term contract. A lack of trust had developed between the two organisations and the consultancy team had been downsized and 'consigned to barracks'. The business customer was unaware of the rift and the unnecessary costs it was bearing. This could be considered as a delivery failure by the supplier (the consultancy organisation) or alternatively we could consider it as a failure of the services provider to buy wisely. As we are assessing the service provider here we consider it to be a buying failure.

Commercial, financial, legal and administrative. We have to assess the supplier's behaviour and the level of expectation set by the supplier during the purchasing process. We must look at their response to the service provider's specification of the requirement and their behaviour during the tendering process but we must also consider the supplier's contractual terms and conditions and their financial procedures particularly those associated with budgets, orders, charges, payments and cost monitoring. Is the contract easy to understand? Is the supplier happy to change the wording of the contract? Perhaps it has been possible to agree a back-to-back contract with the supplier such that they accept the same terms and SLAs as the primary service provider has with the business so minimising the commercial risk. Perhaps the service provider has agreed to provide loan equipment or access to other facilities in the event of a crisis so that the service provider can offer more value to the business. There was a term known as 'stiffing' circulating a few years ago which specifically related to the exploitation of licensing terms and conditions by suppliers: organisations on the receiving end of this practice felt that they had been put into a corner. Have there been any unforeseen implications with regard to any licence or service-level upgrades? What are the cost implications of upgrades (new processor or seats). Has the relationship been influenced positively or negatively in any way by a contractual clause? Are billing and payment arrangements working satisfactorily? Are there any legal exposures between the two parties? Perhaps there is a specialist in-house advisor for trade customers or access to training for certain channels.

People, organisation and governance. How transparent is the organisational structure and governance model of the supplier to the services provider and vice versa? Does the supplier's corporate culture match that of the service provider and that of the business? Does the new supplier bring additional ability, attitude and leadership of some kind? Sometimes suppliers appear and disappear and their ability to add value is never exploited; should the business become more aware of the skills of the supplier in order to increase business value? Are the employment policies of the supplier ethical and consistent with those of the business and the service provider?

Product or service definition. How successful was the supplier's approach to developing an understanding of the service provider's requirement? How successfully did it approach the product or service design phase? Did it embrace the concept of core, actual and augmented product? Did the supplier establish a long-term vision in the minds of the service provider? Did the service provider have a clear view of the benefits associated with the product or service and is there a clear development plan and product upgrade path? What kind of warranty is provided?

Product or service delivery. Each of the bought-in products or services could change our overall perception of performance of the primary service provider. How well is the product or service being delivered? Where does the responsibility for the supplier's performance lie and how are these responsibilities being executed? Who is responsible for contract administration and change management? Are there regular performance reviews of service against a SLA? Are we concerned about the reliability of supply, of the quality of the support (e.g. onsite, telephone, online, web-based, training, documentation) and the assessment of the risks associated with the bought-in products and services? Is the business affected by the delivery of the service by the supplier and is it happy with the quality of the product or service?

Bought-in products and services. How are the supplier's subcontractor and supplier management relationships? Do these arrangements create any limitations on the service being experienced by the service provider or the business? How far back down the supply chain do we need to go with our assessment?

Security. Can all organisations in the IT supply chain be trusted with our business? Do our policies extend into their organisation and to their subcontractors and if not why not? Is the local legislation consistent with our own and sufficiently punitive in the event of transgression or non-compliance? Do all organisations in the IT supply chain have a security policy and allocate responsibility at board level? Do they all take information security and non-disclosure seriously? Are the intellectual assets of the business safe from all of the suppliers in the IT supply chain?

Technology. What technical solutions is the supplier bringing to the business? What is the scope of their vision? Do they bring a sector-specific leadership which can provide a competitive advantage? Is this technology likely to be an asset or a hindrance in the long term?

The business may have a coherent technical strategy that is appropriate to the market in which it operates. Are we happy with the controls that are being exercised to prevent a supplier unwittingly importing hardware or software that is inconsistent with the technical architecture required by the business?

Finally we may wish to compare and chart all of the main suppliers. Each will have a completed assessment of its own and each will have a value for its total business experience and the arithmetic mean of which may be the total business experience of the service provider or the score for bought-in products and services. These are the values that will be compared on a radar diagram as shown in Figure 3.20. In this real example, supplier 6 is new and is being evaluated as a possible replacement for supplier 3 where a number of difficulties are being experienced.

Leadership of bought-in products and services

Leadership of the buying of services is often under-valued. The people involved in these activities should ideally be the budget holders of the part of the organisation with the requirement or be working very closely with those budget holders. They should also bring skills and experience of the sector such that buying decisions and good management prevail. Most commercial services providers buy in some of their products and services and they are generally very good at it. Increasingly most internal services providers now do the same. Unfortunately it is not all good news and this is often an area where those who fail in other fields end up or where people start out their careers. Most mistakes are made early in the project lifecycle placing the success of a project at risk from the outset or

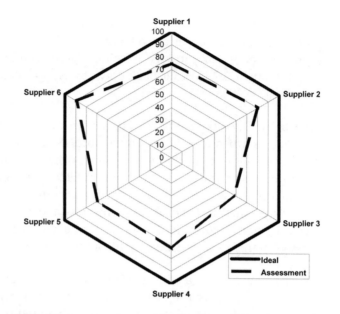

FIGURE 3.20 *Comparing the total business experience from multiple suppliers*

committing the business or service provider to receive poor service for a long period or at least until there is a real prospect of being able to invite new bids to replace the supplier.

'Closeness to the business' is achieved by developing a supplier policy that encourages agility through innovation and flexibility by being able to call upon the best industry specialists as required. This will also reduce cost and increase quality. Leadership could come from the IT services provider or from the business. In the final analysis the initiative always comes from the business if the IT services provider is considered to be failing (i.e. the services provider is outsourced, replaced or competition is introduced).

Security

In Figure 3.13 we looked at the scope of the legal framework affecting IT and showed that it extended beyond the core IT processes. In this section we take another perspective. Almost all businesses would rank security as being critical and yet in many of these businesses we have information security operating within an IT context rather than within a business security context: information security has thus become an IT-focused activity and therefore less relevant to the business. Now that security is so central to business there has to be a way to reposition information security so that it too is more relevant. We have to consider how we can make information security more business-focused than ever before. We therefore consider security at two levels: business security and information security.

The ISO/IEC standard for information security is a star amongst British and international standards but cannot operate within a vacuum.

Perhaps a means of addressing this apparent imbalance is addressed in the following. The argument is that some things should be elevated to the business level but in all areas the IT service provider will be a major contributor. This is an attempt to separate those risks which must involve business leaders because they are big enough to threaten the whole company and those that require diligence or strict adherence to controls within IT. It is not a coincidence that the headings reflect the structure and clauses of the international standard as it is currently implemented but the separation of business and information security is new.

Business security

It is important that business leaders focus on the macro-aspects whilst ensuring that the roles and responsibilities exist to ensure that the appropriate information security and IT controls are properly applied. By separating the macro- from the micro-aspects we can ensure that business and IT work in a coordinated way. The major business aspects of security are as follows.

Business security policy. There is not so much a need for a dry statement of compliance but for something that can more appropriately be used to make everyone associated with the business aware of how seriously the organisation regards the matter. This will not just focus on IT security policies but on the broad security issues of the day. The world in which we work and do business is becoming increasingly global and increasingly hostile: shareholders, employees, suppliers and customers must be made aware of the importance that the organisation attaches to every aspect of security, that it is involved in the associated decision making and that it provides the people and funds to appropriately protect the business.

Just consider two possibilities. The first is an actual information security policy:

> This information security policy is designed to protect business information and IT assets. The policy is designed to provide measures to protect these assets from any organisation, group, or individual who may wish to access, remove, or destroy such assets by whatever means. Control objectives and controls will be determined by the information security committee, membership of which will be published from time to time....

This was followed by an expansion of the various subsets of security policy dealing with compliance, data protection and data privacy, business continuity management, education and training on information security and the consequences of information security violations.

Now consider the following business security policy:

> It is the policy of this business to take measures to protect its people, its assets (including information and intellectual property), and its business capabilities against all perceived risks. This policy is the responsibility of the CEO and will benefit every business unit, business function, supplier, and customer.

How is someone in the business likely to react to the first? Most would probably consider that it was something being done by the IT service provider and that it was not a business responsibility. In the case of the second example however no one in the business (or in an internal or external IT services organisation) would be in any doubt as to the intent, the ownership and the scope. Most people would consider the first to be subservient to the second or to exist within the context of the second. They would be quite correct but in most organisations the second does not exist.

Business assets. There should be an inventory of the physical assets and stock of the business. There should be consistency between this information and information held elsewhere, for example in the case of value of such assets this will be consistent with information held in the financial accounts. Plans, technical specifications, supplier information etc. should also be recorded where appropriate.

There is a need to introduce policy and guidelines to protect the IPR or intellectual assets of the business. This will cover all assets and not be confined to copyright law. All employees, contractors and third parties must sign confidentiality agreements. Third parties (including customers and suppliers) requiring access to either the business premises or the business network should sign third-party agreements for the same reason. There is also a need for the business to ensure that it does not infringe upon the copyright (including performing rights) of others.

Most contracts will have a clause covering the ownership of the IPR of the parties to the contract. The contract will address both the ownership of assets existing before the assignment and those created during the assignment.

When we mention intellectual assets we think perhaps of trade secrets, blueprints, recipes, formulae etc. Quite often businesses are just as protective towards company records such as customer contact details, orders, sales pipelines etc.

Business risk assessment. Having acknowledged that the business will always be exposed to risk, there should be a regular and robust review of the risks that the business is exposed to such that it is able to understand the likelihood and impact of these occurring and consider what measures might be introduced. Technology risks would be factored into all business risks and the IT assets, infrastructure and business information must be recognised as making the business vulnerable to certain possibilities. Even in the aftermath of 9/11 it was the author's experience that it was the IT people that were taking the debate to most businesses. It is through risk assessment that business leaders will be involved in making the judgements and the contribution we all need them to make.

Sharing business security intelligence. Businesses cannot hope to know enough about the security risks they face without consulting with others outside their organisations. Businesses must take advice from organisations that are likely to have more intelligence about security threats than they have or from organisations prepared to pool or exchange this information. Organisations, including governments, that may have intelligence about threats must make this information available via appropriate channels to all businesses so that risks can be reassessed and if necessary new measures can be introduced. Once the principle has been established at the business level, it can be made to operate at all other levels within the business including at the information security level.

Business and organisational responsibilities. As in all aspects of management it is important to clearly assign responsibility, but security requires a lot of diligence on detailed matters and it has many facets. The business must satisfy itself that it has the people, skills and experience in place to deal with the measures that need to be taken and that the roles are clear.

Business protection from malicious intent. The fact is that there are a lot of unpleasant people and organisations around who want to do harm to your business. On the menu we have terrorism, extortion, sabotage, theft, fraud, vandalism, denial of service, unauthorised access, masquerading as others, identity theft, system penetration, voice and data network security and the consequences of each. These consequences could lead to theft of intellectual property, loss of service, loss of facility, loss of money, loss of assets and loss of business. Some businesses or management teams may be more at risk than others because of the nature of their activities but present-day terrorism is less discriminating.

Business continuity management. Business leaders must be satisfied that the business can continue to operate after a major incident. They may call upon their experts in particular areas but this has to come together at the top of the business so that the appropriate amount of funding can be made available. It will ensure that disaster recovery plans are in place to cover the most likely eventualities. It will satisfy itself that business continuity plans are feasible. The business will drive or review the risk assessment process to understand the impact and likelihood, controls and funding.

Business supplier management. Most organisations now have to operate in the context of an extended enterprise. There will be suppliers, subcontractors, partner organisations, outsourced service providers, full-time and contract staff. Businesses must consider carefully the risks they may be exposed to as a result of these relationships. Some will be IT related, some will not. It is interesting to note that it is currently very difficult to find a major financial services company in the UK that does not have a service operation outside the regions of the world covered by data protection legislation (i.e. USA, Europe and the UK) and this is a sector where controls are supposed to be at their highest. This is not a xenophobic outcry, it is the simple truth that every financial services organisation assumes that the threat of the sack will deter employees in these countries from stealing personal data and selling it, even though this is not a criminal offence outside of the USA, EU and UK and these people will be able to retire in comfort on relatively small amounts of money compared with those in the west. Personal data is sacrosanct but small fry compared with the potential impact of some of the risks being taken by companies in sensitive sectors exploiting globalisation by operating in countries with few legal frameworks.

Business compliance. The growth in UK and international legislation continues and compliance becomes an increasingly important issue for all companies and one which affects a company's ability to trade. Although IT underpins all business activities and the IT services provider will be involved in all aspects of compliance matters, it is fundamentally a business responsibility.

Sarbanes-Oxley 2002 (US) applies to US companies, to all companies listed on the US stock exchanges and to foreign subsidiaries of US-listed companies. It is a reaction to regulatory, audit and reporting failures at Enron and WorldCom and is designed to tighten up corporate financial reporting and improve transparency in order to strengthen and restore investor confidence in companies listed on the US markets. The act expands the responsibilities of the audit committee, it allows the work of the auditor to be investigated, it increases the amount of financial disclosure required from companies, it requires a full disclosure of all conflicts of interest, it forces corporate attorneys to report their clients for securities violations, it prohibits international accounting firms from providing lucrative consulting services to their clients, it makes CEOs and CFOs criminally liable for any misleading statements in published accounts and dramatically increases penalties for companies and their officers (with sentences of up to 25 years and personal fines of $5 million for non-compliance). Companies are introducing new financial and reporting processes and documenting the IT controls they have in place to ensure compliance. Section 404 deals with the integrity of the information on which auditors' reports are based. The UK Companies Act 2006 includes similar requirements.

Business data and privacy. Data on individuals must be fairly and lawfully processed in accordance with the Data Protection Act 1998 (UK) or similar legislation in force locally. This includes not transferring such data to countries lacking adequate legal protection (i.e. not having legislation similar to this act). Individuals have a right to know what the personal information is being used for, organisations must obtain positive consent in order to hold the information and the information commissioner must be informed of the intent. There is also the European Privacy Directive 2002 (EU). Service suppliers and businesses must delete or 'anonymise' personal traffic data after it is no longer needed, obtain consent before marketing by email, tell customers how their data is to be processed and places limitations on what can be done with location data and cookies. Failure to comply is a criminal offence. In addition the Freedom of Information Act 2005 (UK) means that the public has a right to be told if public authorities hold information about them.

The US also has data protection legislation and there is also the California Breach Law. This requires that anyone doing business in California must notify their customers if any computerised information held on them has been acquired or is believed to have been acquired by an unauthorised third party. It is this law that possibly encouraged a UK bank to announce publicly that they had lost a laptop computer containing customer account details.

Some would consider data protection to be an IT issue and as a result it is not taken seriously, even though failure to comply is a criminal offence. This is why today we have organisations, even in the most sensitive sectors (i.e. healthcare and financial services), routinely transferring and processing data in countries that do not have data protection legislation with little consideration for UK or EU data protection legislation.

Environmental information regulations (UK/Europe). This gives the public the right to ask for environmental data on topics such as pollution, carbon output, radiation, genetically modified organisms etc. There will be implications in terms of information management in the manufacturing sectors in particular. Environmental controls and legislation is likely to increase in coming years.

Specific legislation for the business sector. Each sector whether this is financial services, food processing, healthcare, transport and distribution etc. will have its own legislation that must be complied with. Clearly this publication could not begin to provide a complete list of all of the legislation covering all sectors but IT service providers must be aware of the sector-specific legislation that applies in order to endure that compliance is built into systems where appropriate.

Business incident management. The business needs to be aware of any breach or incident immediately in order for investigations to have a greater chance of success. Breaches will also be analysed over time to look at trends and as a source of input to risk (re)assessment and security investment decisions. The business review of breaches will include all breaches including those in the information security domain (see the following section).

Information security

Within the context of the business security policies above, there are many areas where the diligence specifically of the IT service provider is needed. These will involve further risk assessment in order to identify the impact and likelihood of an occurrence and to develop controls in all areas of IT and telecommunications.

This will require security policies and procedures specifically for the information environment. There will be access rules (internal and third party) and management information, for example records of breaches and incidents remembering that as many as 60% of information security breaches are behind the firewall. All policies must be kept up to date with changes to the law and changes of practice and threat.

Just as responsibilities will have been defined for business security, there will be a need for information security responsibilities to be clearly defined. Overall responsibility may already be clear but the responsibility for each information asset, information security process and authorisation process needs to be allocated.

Information security risk assessment. Although addressed at the business level the risk assessment will be repeated at the information security level and major risks and controls will be raised with the business for prioritisation. During this process the IT service provider should have the same access to incidents and breaches as the business in order to properly assess trends and risks.

Information asset management. Information assets include physical objects, software (and licenses), IPR, information itself and maybe even people. Service providers must maintain an inventory, assign ownership for the assets and ensure that they are only used in acceptable ways. Information asset management requires an inventory of these physical and other assets by asset classification type. Physical assets will be labelled. A key to managing information assets and the risks associated with retention is the need to ensure that we do nothing to invalidate a warranty: equipment must be maintained and software must be upgraded.

Information personnel security. Information technology underpins all processes and so people wishing to work in IT should be screened when recruited to check that there is no history that would make the applicant unsuitable. The employer has a duty of care to exercise a right to vet potential employees to reduce business risk. All employees must be made aware of their duty to the business through confidentiality agreements, IPR, privacy, use of assets etc. and must be asked to sign agreements to this effect. As in all other fields if we want people to succeed we need to provide training and this is true of information security. Disciplinary procedures must exist for breaches and be seen to be used.

Leavers should be processed to ensure that they are reminded of their ongoing obligations to the company after they cease to become employees.

Information security requires that third-party contracts with suppliers, contract services organisations and outsourced and offshore services organisations protect the business from exposures to fraud, theft, malicious intent, data misuse etc. by the employees of these companies. If it continues to be difficult to enforce compliance or penalties on offshore organisations outside of the UK/EU/US zones then offshore supplier policies should be reassessed.

Physical access and environmental security of information assets. Within the context of the business security policies and procedures there will be considerations about access to buildings and the risk of theft, malicious damage and sabotage etc. but within the context of information security we have to concern ourselves with flooding, secure power supplies, fire precautions, cabling and WIFI security.

There will be physical access controls to areas where servers or other departmental or company-wide processors are located. This will involve the control of keys, clear desk policy and the movement of assets. Offsite equipment is particularly vulnerable to misuse but controls should be applied rather than restricting the use of equipment needed by people who are required to work offsite.

Information systems access control. We can no longer provide a secure service by merely protecting the boundaries because there are all manner of ways of gaining access to the network either wirelessly or via small personal devices such as USB drives or when synchronising telephones or PDAs.

There must be an access control policy and user access management with responsibilities made clear to all users and third parties that require access; there may be network access control, operating system access control and application system access control. There may be constant monitoring of system access and use, mobile computing, remote access or teleworking and internet and ecommerce controls from trusted, semi-trusted and un-trusted locations.

Operating procedures will reflect security requirements including incident management, the separation of duties, system planning and acceptance, housekeeping, backup and recovery, offsite storage of back-up data, network management including firewalls, email management, voice network management (switchboards, mobile, VoIP etc.), media handling and security, cryptography and exchanges of information and software (must be clear of unintentional data), protection against malicious software, SPAM filters, software for credit card fraud and the availability of forensics skills and the preservation of audit trails of breaches that will enable successful prosecutions to be obtained in court. IT forensics become key to the collection of evidence.

Information systems acquisition, development and maintenance. There should be a thorough understanding of the business requirement and a sound risk analysis. Security will be a key consideration for all new systems: input data validation, processing controls, message authentication, output data validation etc. There may be a need for cryptographic controls, special requirements for the security of system files or security during development and support processes. All proposals from third parties should be assessed against these criteria as well as the match to the business need, cost, ability to deliver etc.

Information systems compliance. There are specific areas of compliance that will play straight into the IT arena such as any legislation addressed at spammers, for example the Can Spam Act of 2003 (US) requires that any unsolicited commercial email messages are clearly labelled and offer the recipient the ability to opt out. In all other respects information systems must comply with the business security requirements for the appropriate business sector.

Change management. The change management process considers risk introduced by change vis-à-vis the security needs of the business. Change management must consider the threats that can be remedied at the time of the change. Patch management is part of a change management and release management process for software upgrades.

Leadership of security

'Closeness to the business' is achieved by ensuring that the responsibility for security must be with the business, not IT, and it must embrace corporate security, business units, the technical fields and all aspects of compliance with legislation. The IT service provider will take up responsibility for information security within the context of the corporate security role thus from an IT perspective there is dual leadership.

Technology

This will quite intentionally be the shortest section of this book; it is the focus of our attention and yet in some respects it is the aspect which is least under our control. As few of us actually create the technology the only control we have is the choice of what we as service providers or business managers deploy. The technical platform or the technology itself is the most intimidating aspect of computing for the business manager and the most intriguing for technologists. Neither situation is helpful to the business. We are talking here about the hardware and software infrastructure. Let us look at what is important from a business perspective and then think about how the IT service provider might respond.

Scope of the vision

The scope of the technology vision and the scope of the actual deployment is manifested within the organisation's IT strategy. Many organisations still operate in a silo-like manner, each function or division looking to meet its own needs. Sometimes this is appropriate if the organisation is federal in nature but often it is a sign of limited vision and a limited vision can sometimes lead to limited opportunity. Alternatively we see organisations where there is an enterprise perspective and shared services. We can only decide which is the most appropriate if the service provider is 'close to the business' and these decisions are being made with a full understanding of the implications.

To maximise the business value of a technology infrastructure it is important to develop, document and discuss the proposed strategy. This encourages debate, increases understanding and helps to build the business case for investment. Properly documented it can encourage discussion about the alternative models, features and the extent of investment.

Technology deployed

What the business will expect is not just any technology but an industry standard environment, consistent with the rest of the organisation, key suppliers and major customers. If we fail to adopt an industry standard environment we may be sacrificing easy connectivity with some external organisations in the extended enterprise or ecosystem on which the business is becoming increasingly dependent.

The business is likely to want feature-rich products rather than sparse or expensive bespoke developments unless these create substantial competitive advantage. Most businesses will object to the cost of maintaining system software at the latest release levels and yet will not thank the IT service provider for an unstable, fragile, obsolete infrastructure that has lost the confidence of the business.

One of the characteristics of the latest technology is that it is always easier to use and has a higher utility value than previous generations of technology. As has always been the case with IT, there are opportunities to increase automation, increase business benefits and reduce business costs. Finally by choosing the technology carefully we can expect a significant degree of future-proofing.

Introducing new technology

The IT service provider will maintain or upgrade what it has to avoid obsolescence. From time to time it will replace what it has with a new generation of technology. Replacement technology is often presented to business as a necessary cost on a like-for-like basis, that is as a replacement for a fully depreciated asset where the maintenance costs may be rising. The common assumption here is that the replacement benefits the service provider by reducing operating costs but in many of these cases the replacement technology may offer additional business benefits which rarely get exploited until commonplace elsewhere.

It is interesting to observe that technological innovation is frequently used in ways that were not anticipated by the vendor. This is because all innovation is viewed from today's perspective but over a short period of time that perspective is revised based on what is now possible rather than being based on what we have previously always done.

Technology leadership

All organisations need technology leadership. Technology leadership is recognised by appropriate technical strategies that drive changes in technical direction consistent with main market opinion. In other words the previous state and the final state are both main market. The arbitrator of what is main market has in the past been the CIO.

Interestingly both before and after the change the successful business will have technology that is consistent with or anticipates that deployed by the rest of the organisation, key suppliers and major customers. For this reason the business is increasingly becoming the arbitrator: the business is beginning to provide leadership for technology. If the business fails to display this leadership there is a danger that it will become isolated technologically. If it introduces the changes too early the business will pay the financial penalty of being an innovator. If the business introduces the changes too late there may be a penalty in terms of lost business.

Relevance in this instance is achieved by maintaining or enhancing the connectivity with the main market and the ecosystem. This also increases agility in that new requirements can be addressed quickly within an industry standard architecture. The CIO can ensure that the business is made aware of technical developments so that investment mistakes are not made. Where there may be competitive advantage in deploying a technology before the main market, the business and CIO must jointly assess the risks. This creates the 'closeness' that will ensure success.

4 Bringing it all Together

During this chapter we explain how easily we can expose the strengths and weaknesses of service providers, identify different styles of service provider and build performance improvement programmes.

SUMMARISING THE ASSESSMENT CRITERIA

Figure 4.1 summarises how we might quickly assess the service engine of an IT service provider and how to derive a value for brand equity, core product or service and the total business experience. The subject and aspects broadly correspond to the headings in 'The detail of the analysis' section of the previous chapter but with some practice you will not need the book, just the charts. Score each aspect out of 100 and calculate an overall average for each subject, the score for brand equity, for core product or service and for the total business experience. The rules for the calculations are shown in the appropriate cell of the table.

	Subject	Aspect	Max	Actual
1	Business and sector awareness	Knowledge of the macro-environment	100	
		Knowledge of the meso-environment	100	
		Knowledge of the micro-environment	100	
		Critical information set	100	
		Assumptions, opportunities and threats	100	
		Budget	100	
		Leadership	100	
		Average	100	
2	Marketing and communications	Brand	100	
		Products and markets	100	
		Communications strategy	100	
		IT strategy framework	100	
		Strategic data layer	100	
		Budget	100	
		Leadership	100	
		Average	100	
3	Sales and value-add	Sales strategy	100	
		Sales management	100	
		Creation of business value	100	
		Investment portfolio or sales pipeline	100	
		Budget	100	
		Leadership	100	
		Average	100	
4	Commercial, Financial, Legal and Administrative	Commercial and financial management	100	
		Legal and administration management	100	
		Budget	100	
		Leadership	100	
		Average	100	
5	People, Organisation, and Governance	Organisation structure	100	
		Governance framework	100	
		Corporate culture	100	
		Individual and group effectiveness	100	
		Budget	100	
		Leadership	100	
		Average	100	

B	Brand equity (sum of 1–5)/5		100	
6	Product and service definition	Understanding the requirement	100	
		Product and service design	100	
		Build versus buy	100	
		Infrastructure planning	100	
		Budget	100	
		Leadership	100	
		Average	100	
7	Product and service delivery	Operations management	100	
		Programme and project management	100	
		Quality management	100	
		Budget	100	
		Leadership	100	
		Average	100	
8	Bought-in products and services	Supplier's business awareness	100	
		Supplier's marketing and communications	100	
		Supplier's sales and value-add	100	
		Supplier's commercial, financial, legal and administrative	100	
		Supplier's people, organisation and governance	100	
		Supplier's product and service definition	100	
		Supplier's product and service delivery	100	
		Supplier's bought-in products and services	100	
		Supplier's security	100	
		Supplier's technology	100	
		Budget	100	
		Leadership		
		Average	100	
9	Security	Business security	100	
		Information security	100	
		Budget	100	
		Leadership	100	
		Average	100	
10	Technology	Scope of the vision	100	
		Technology deployed	100	
		Introducing new technology	100	
		Budget	100	
		Leadership	100	
		Average	100	
C	Core product or service (sum of 6–10)/5		100	
A	Total business experience (B × C/100)		100	

FIGURE 4.1 *Scoring the assessment*

EXAMPLE ASSESSMENTS

Figure 4.2–4.10 shows assessments of real IT services organisations encountered during some of the author's assignments. They will remain anonymous and we do not cover them in any detail but they illustrate the strengths and weaknesses of the various organisations. It often surprises people how much the profiles vary from one organisation to another. The more work we do in this area the clearer it becomes that although we can all learn from best practice, any 'one size fits all' approach to how an IT services organisation should work is inappropriate. It also explains why simplistic IT performance improvement programmes frequently fail.

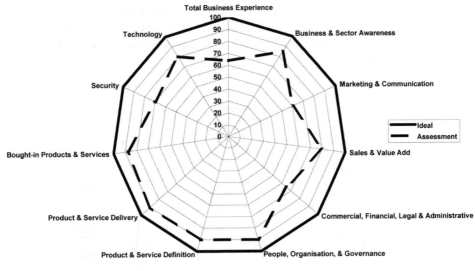

FIGURE 4.2 *Assessment example one*

Example one (Figure 4.2) is the profile of an internal IT services provider to an international investment banking organisation. Business awareness is strong but not as strong as it would like. Being a bank it is never happy with security or the commercial and financial aspects but the information gathered in this analysis formed the basis of a global performance improvement programme that included communication, value-add and the technology platform.

FIGURE 4.3 *Assessment example two*

Example two (Figure 4.3) is the profile of a commercial IT services provider. Its strengths are in winning business rather than in delivery. The service provider is usually fronted by another organisation that sees this supplier as a specialist in its field but with a poor delivery record: one has to ask why. The poor delivery has a detrimental effect on the total business experience of those businesses that buy or resell the services of this company.

FIGURE 4.4   *Assessment example three*

Example three (Figure 4.4) is the profile of an internal IT department in the public sector. It is really quite good at the technical stuff but does not understand the core business and is not liked by the business because it fails to communicate, is not seen to add value and its commercial processes are non-existent. In fact this was to be sold at the privatisation of the industry and it had to be developed into a commercial IT services organisation for the industry sector. This was probably the biggest transformation of its kind. By the time the business was sold the profile was much more balanced with all of the brand equity deficiencies (sector awareness, marketing and communication, sales and value-add, commercial, financial, legal and administrative) having been addressed. It was interesting to note the enthusiasm of the business for the changes and the improvement to their total business experience. This was only possible because of the quality of the people which even in the 'before' state as illustrated above was seen to be strong.

Example four (Figure 4.5) is the profile of a product-based start-up business and the skills reflect the skills of the founding partners. The founding partners were shown this assessment and they thought they could survive and grow their business without bringing in new skills; the business went into liquidation 12 months later.

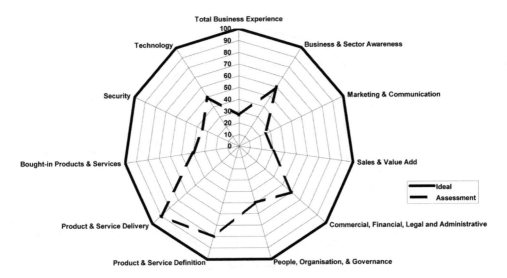

FIGURE 4.5   *Assessment example four*

FIGURE 4.6   *Assessment example five*

Example five (Figure 4.6) is the profile of an offshore consultancy and development organisation. They were cheap, good at selling, quick to invoice, but many customers did not feel that they got what they paid for without spending as much again managing the supplier. They are still in business, growing rapidly and, as far as we can see, still failing to deliver. In the case of one major UK consultancy contract they have been side-lined, although because they are subcontractors this is not apparent to the business customer. The problems centre on their apparent inability to adequately analyse a business problem and propose an acceptable business solution.

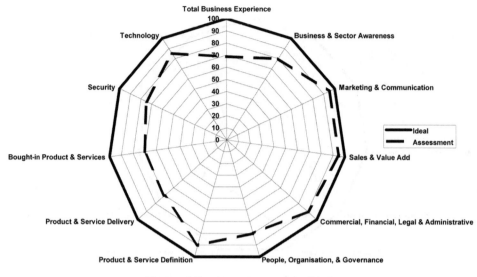

FIGURE 4.7   *Assessment example six*

Example six (Figure 4.7) is a profile of a software and services organisation. It was competent commercially and its sales and marketing skills were driving growth but there were issues around product and service delivery as well as supplier selection and supplier management. The effect this had on the total business experience provided the justification for bringing improvement to these areas.

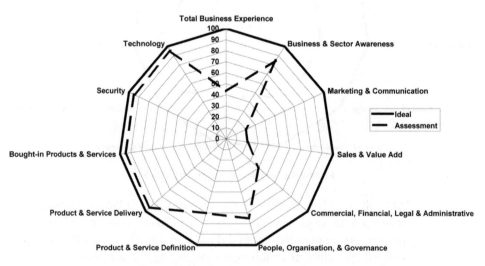

FIGURE 4.8   *Assessment example seven*

Example seven (Figure 4.8) is the profile is of a large internal IT services provider to the engineering division of a major publicly owned corporation. The subsequent and very successful performance improvement programme led eventually to this organisation taking over the delivery of IT services to the whole of the corporation.

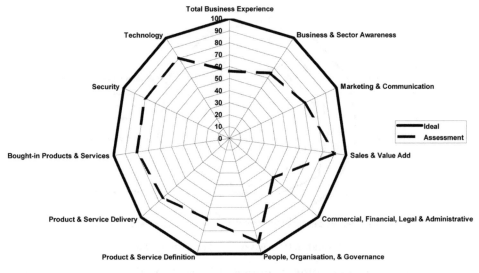

FIGURE 4.9   *Assessment example eight*

Example eight (Figure 4.9) is the profile of a major global outsourced services provider. This organisation is rather successful but it was weak at marketing and very weak in the commercial area frequently taking on loss-making business and failing to file company accounts. On the delivery side it succeeded as many times as it failed but its real weakness was in failing to develop compelling IT strategies for business customers and failing to suitably define the business requirement. Its strength was in delivering the same at a lower cost which was in part a result of its supplier alliances and in part of its ability to manage its people better than they had been managed before (i.e. using fewer staff).

The final profile (Figure 4.10) is that of an internal IT department of a retail bank. Here we have two views, the first as seen by the management and staff of the services provider and the second by their business customers and users. During an assessment it is normal to seek as many views as possible both from within the services organisation, from its customer base and even from suppliers and the end customer if this is appropriate and consolidate them to provide a single value on each of the ten scales. In this case the services organisation was the client and they asked us to show the comparison between the internal IT view and the business view. The services provider was disappointed by the results overall but pleased that the business rated them higher than they rated themselves in most areas. In particular the services provider was disappointed by the business assessment of its awareness of the banking sector. It is easy to assume that the internal services provider will always understand the sector in which it operates, but it is not unusual for external organisations to be more aware and to work harder at keeping this knowledge up to date. This particular internal IT department had arrangements in place with a number of external services providers who the business managers rated more highly than the internal people.

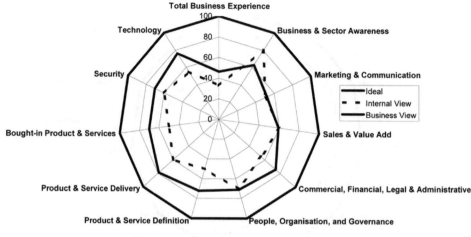

FIGURE 4.10 *Assessment example nine*

In all of these nine examples it is worth noting the value for the total business experience. In every case these were calculated using the formula given above and then validated by the business as being representative of their overall opinion.

BUILDING A PERFORMANCE IMPROVEMENT PLAN

As we identify shortfalls using the service excellence model and the assessment framework for the service engine (scoring the latter in the table of Figure 4.1) we will identify opportunities for improvement. These can be added to the diagram illustrated below (Figure 4.11) so that we can quickly put a structure around a future improvement programme. Priorities can be highlighted so that rather than a 'cause and effect' fishbone diagram, we can consider this to be more of an 'improvements and outcome' diagram.

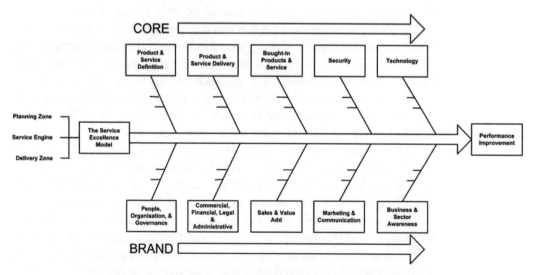

FIGURE 4.11 *The 'improvements and outcome' fishbone diagram*

This enables us to ensure that all ideas are captured (rather than being forgotten) and later prioritised. As for business investment decisions, we can consider the cost, benefits, risk, impact and dependency before deciding on the performance improvement programme. The normal situation is that this kind of assessment and improvement planning will be conducted as part of an internal drive for increased effectiveness. It could be driven by the IT service provider or by the business and repeated on a regular basis. Even though the underlying technology, the organisation and the suppliers may change, we can still measure the total business experience. Questionnaires may come and go but the assessment framework for the service engine is a stable model suitable for tracking performance over the long term. It also absorbs complexity and automatically adapts to the latest business and technical situations. As expectations are raised in terms of what is possible, the 'ideal' level of 100% in fact moves outwards and we establish a new norm for the basis of assessing the services received; this means that the 'assessment' will appear to have diminished even though the delivered service may not have changed.

A business in the financial services sector had experienced massive growth and in turn this had created pressure points within IT as that had expanded to meet demand. The business wanted an independent assessment of the situation and some recommendations as to what had to be done. This was a rapidly changing environment employing very capable people where ideas flowed very quickly. To reach consensus would not only require a good analysis of the situation but a process that would enable consensus to be reached. Although the scope of this work was initially restricted to Europe and centred on London this was soon changed so that it became a global study culminating in a workshop in New York for all vice-presidents throughout the world. The approach meant that the work could be undertaken globally within reasonable timescales. The frameworks provided an effective structure for communicating the assessment and recommendations so that unambiguous discussion could be held and consensus could be achieved. Finally the process identified cause and effect and so interdependencies were easy to manage. Most of the vice-presidents present at the workshop had contributed previously in various ways but were now invited to review and prioritise all of the recommendations and were allowed to delete or add new ones. The most valuable outcome from the workshop was the clear consensus on what had to be done. The action plan had the full support of the global management team. It became clear during this assignment that the conclusions that were eventually reached would not have been reached or would not have been so compelling if the assessment had only taken into account the normal considerations of IT planning, design and delivery. The improvement programme in fact consisted of some 23 prioritised and separate activities spread across ten concurrent workstreams.

An overseas IT product vendor needed to both scale the business to handle a greater UK workload and achieve compliance with several international standards in order to meet the terms of a major new contract. At the outset there was concern about the additional overhead costs of the compliance on top of the additional workload. We were chosen to assist because we could demonstrate that we could introduce both radical service improvement and procedural compliance (i.e. we were seen as being able to deliver Big Q and Little Q). The assessment identified all potential areas for improvement, not just within the UK but across the whole of the supply chain or ecosystem. Processes and procedures were developed that were compliant with the appropriate standards (ISO 20000, ISO 17799 and ISO 13485) and these would be implemented globally. Deployment and installation plans, compliant procedures, resourcing plans, resource estimates, performance measures and cost of quality measures were developed. It was interesting that although the business customer had stipulated that ITIL was to be used it drew heavily on project management methods and templates for deployment. Instead we chose to use release management processes which created massive resource, cost and time savings. The net effect of the assignment was that not only would existing service gaps be closed but rather than being under pressure to meet the new delivery schedules the business would now easily cope with the additional workload with a minimal increase in resources. In fact one unexpected outcome was that we were able to develop a flexible demand driven resourcing model that would allow the business to take on even more work and still deliver to a customer-driven schedule. This was seen to provide additional competitive advantage which could drive further orders.

CIRCUMSTANCES AND ORGANISATIONS REQUIRING SPECIAL CONSIDERATION

There are other circumstances and organisations worthy of special consideration when considering service excellence. The special circumstances include the transition from one service provider to another and during mergers and acquisitions. The organisations worthy of special consideration include the public sector and 'not for profit' organisations.

Transitioning from one service provider to another

Outsourcing involves the business selling its IT service function to one or more service providers and entering into long-term contracts with those suppliers. In this situation the outsourced service providers frequently manage the transition process after completing the due diligence phase. The service excellence model combined with the assessment framework for the service engine would ensure that every aspect of the service is transitioned without risk or duplication and at the same time the service provider is able to agree an agenda for change to improve the total business experience.

A variation on this is where one service provider is replaced by another. Again, the service excellence model and the assessment framework for the service engine will identify the opportunities for improvement and define the scope and priorities of what has to be considered during a transition process.

During mergers and acquisitions

The immediate short-term objective in all mergers or acquisitions is to secure the resources in order to guarantee the continuity of the business being acquired (at least until we know what is intended for it); the acquired business must continue to trade (legally). To achieve this we need to approach the due diligence phase in a structured and rigorous way. By undertaking a full assessment of IT service provision within the new business using the service excellence model and the assessment framework for the service engine we can fully understand what is being acquired, the strengths, the weaknesses and the risks. IT management should pay particular attention to people, assets, facilities, intellectual property, suppliers, software licensing and compliance.

As soon as possible, we must understand the business intent for the acquisition. Incorrect assumptions at this stage could prove to be expensive. Typical strategies might be as follows.

- Wholly absorb the acquired business.
- Run the acquired business as an independent subsidiary.
- Retaining a part of the acquired business either absorbing this into the business or into an existing subsidiary or running it as an independent subsidiary. The remainder to be sold as either as a collection of assets (possibly combined with others that the business wishes to dispose of) or as some kind of trading entity (again drawing assets from this acquisition and possibly combining with others).

Each of these requires a different kind of IT strategy, action plan and investment case. Once the business intent and the IT strategy are clear we must plan the transition. Just like an outsourcing arrangement an acquisition must be transitioned. This must both reflect the priorities identified during due diligence and the actions needed to achieve the objectives of the acquisition itself.

On the technology front we must consider whether it is worth harmonising the infrastructure to facilitate better connectivity with the acquiring organisation. Intuitively we assume this is always going to be necessary but clearly this will not be the case if it is to be operated at arms length from the rest of the business. We must ensure that our acquisition is secure and that a business continuity programme is in place and that it is fit for purpose. We must understand the processes for defining and developing strategy. We must identify existing gaps and current investment plans and programmes and intervene where necessary. Current levels of service may give rise to concern and we may wish to put in place some kind of performance improvement program. We may also wish to homogenise the reporting metrics with those in other parts of the business in order to provide meaningful comparisons of performance. We must look at the people, organisation and governance to ensure that we have control. Fundamentally the transition must also motivate those people to be retained: this may mean winning hearts and minds; it may mean putting down some markers for performance improvement. Any actions on the administrative, legal and financial aspects must be addressed. Change of ownership can raise licensing issues that must not be ignored. Any shortcomings in the ability of the IT service organisation to either add value or communicate must be tackled immediately as these are areas where the acquired business will see an immediate benefit. Finally we must be aware that if the acquired business is in a new business sector as a result of some strategy of diversification, we as the acquiring business may know little about the business being acquired. This can present opportunities for the transfer of knowledge but it can also leave us open to criticism that we fail to understand their business. As a consequence we must be cautious when formulating our transition policies to ensure that key sector requirements are addressed.

For IT to make the greatest possible contribution to the acquisition process, it should be involved at the earliest opportunity. Most would now agree with this sentiment but there was a time when this was not the case.

What changed the views of the significance of the role of IT in the acquisition process for one company was when they discovered that the acquired business would soon have neither application systems nor IT infrastructure at which point it would cease to be a 'going concern' and cease trading. According to the terms of the sale, the vendor would allow the acquired business to use its IT systems for a period of six months following the completion of the sale of the business during which time the acquiring business would need to provision replacement systems and infrastructure. The internal IT services organisation of the acquiring business had repeatedly requested to see the terms of the contract of sale but the business failed to respond for several months. By the time the clause in the contract had been found by the IT services provider of the acquiring company it had just three months to find new systems, new hardware and new premises. The story ended happily but needless to say the IT services provider was invited to participate in the due diligence process of every subsequent acquisition made by that business from that time forward.

The public sector

The public sector can be divided into three groups: major government departments (including the police, armed forces and the NHS), local authorities and minor government departments and finally current and former publicly owned but heavily regulated industries (e.g. rail infrastructure, transport operators, energy and water utilities, telecommunications, postal services etc.).

Although they may all be at different stages in their cultural development they are characterised by complex stakeholder relationships. Some may now have a profit motive but the accompanying regulation will mean that they can never be managed in the more straightforward ways of private sector business. Even though salaries may be as high as in other sectors, what can be achieved is often less. Culturally the people in the public sector will usually have a preference for low risk and job security and may be averse to change and aggressive targets. Programme managers beware: you must be able to manage conflicting or qualitative objectives, many stakeholder views and reluctant staff. Government tends to use the larger integrators to deliver change in this sector in the belief that they will have some financial redress if they fail to deliver but effective experienced independent change managers are also needed to ensure that the larger integrators are effectively managed. For these reasons and others, and with reference to the service excellence model, there will always be a major service requirement gap with difficulties both in delivery and planning.

The author was retained to assess the provision of IT services to a major public sector business. Quality assurance accreditations, independent user satisfaction surveys and benchmark comparisons suggested a high standard of IT service was being achieved but the there were concerns at the highest levels of the business that IT would be unable to meet the needs of the business going forward. Using the frameworks described, the overall assessment was very poor in almost every aspect. Performance was clearly being measured against an undemanding service specification defined by the IT service providers rather than against business need or expectation. It was relatively straightforward using the approaches described to propose an improvement programme that would not just address the technical requirements but also the broader business requirements. The IT manager was challenged to deliver the improvement but later the author was recalled and asked to take on this role as an interim manager and also to select a new head of IT. As the changes were to affect all aspects of the service engine everyone in the business became aware of the changes and the benefits associated with the changes. IT engaged the business more effectively at all levels. It engaged the business strategically to understand requirements and

(Continued)

159

(Continued)

to assess new technologies and solutions, managerially by organising itself and communicating more effectively and operationally by improving day-to-day service levels. Costs were reduced quite dramatically and satisfaction ratings (still being measured independently) rose. A new head of IT was selected and appointed and transitioned to take over the department and the ongoing initiatives. This once failing IT department eventually took the lead in IT throughout the group as the business was restructured. The head of IT eventually became the group IT director. This was not just a technology refresh of some kind but a fundamental change in the way that IT served the business that was addressed in a business-focused way and which throughout retained the support of the business in driving through the necessary changes and introducing improvements.

The 'not for profit' sector

This community is changing but inevitably attracts people with high ethics. Although we may be grouping organisations as diverse as charities, membership associations, educational establishments, community groups etc. the common denominator is the need to demonstrate value for money and high ethical standards to the client organisations. Having said this the rules are the same. The service excellence model, the total business experience and the assessment framework for the service engine all apply as for any other business.

When it comes to the improvement programmes 'not for profit' organisations will often have difficulties associated with timescales and funding. The timescales associated with both decisions and funding will generate gaps that will be highlighted by the service excellence model; proposals have to go via whatever governance arrangements are in place for decisions, often the funding is more restricted and sometimes the required funds first have to be raised. In some ways it has much in common with the public sector in terms of stakeholder complexities but with the added problem of this slowness to respond. This means that planning must be better and must anticipate more possible future scenarios so that funding decisions can be made against multiple possibilities. Also change programmes must yield the benefits they were designed to yield if any funding gap is not to be exacerbated.

The author was recently working as a change manager or interim CEO for a large membership organisation where there had been a management failure. The main task was to introduce organisational change and governance improvement within a very short period of time. We wanted to base this restructuring on a better understanding of how the organisation was likely to be functioning in the future

(Continued)

(Continued)

(i.e. based on more modern management practices). We used the IT strategy framework to identify a target architecture (process, infrastructure, systems and data). To deliver the IT changes the organisation would need access to a broader range of IT skills and so during this assignment we also outsourced the IT. The chosen supplier was selected on its ability to deliver what we knew would be critical to the business over the next two years rather than on what IT was doing at the time. We had developed an improvement programme based on an assessment of the needs of the business and the state of IT and so we needed an IT services provider that could inject a strategic element into its support. Interestingly the selected company was already providing similar services to many organisations of this size that had chosen to retain no internal IT resource and so it recognised the importance to their customers of providing a broader skill set and broader business support capability. Understanding the impact that IT would have on the membership organisation also helped when it came to recruiting new senior people because we had a much better idea of what they would be tasked with doing and what skills and experience they would need to have. The main focus on this assignment was not IT but the use of the business-focused IT frameworks which enabled us to work quickly and comprehensively to complete the IT aspects of this task very satisfactorily. Subsequent to the author's involvement the organisation authorised a new investment in technology and so it is moving forward with confidence. From our point of view we also have the satisfaction of knowing that the role of IT, at least in this organisation, will be contextually correct.

WHAT TO EXPECT

'Business-focused IT' is not a theoretical methodology. The approach fits neatly with all other frameworks in as much as they provide the current IT industry view of best practice in the relevant areas of IT activity. ITIL, COBIT and other frameworks can be used to analyse the detail of the IT-focused components of the IT service and where they are used our understanding of IT is improved. What 'business-focused IT' allows us to achieve is to understand where the implementation (or not) of these and all other aspects of service are failing the business and the gaps that are created. It allows us to choose whether or to what extent we wish to close these gaps and how we wish to approach the improvement process.

Where we have been retained to address what has been perceived to be an IT problem we have been able to quickly isolate not just the needs of the business but the causes of business concern, the strengths and weaknesses of IT delivery and the nature of the relationships between the business and IT. If gaps can be identified using the service excellence model then we have to ask if these are likely to be closed by our proposed improvement programme for the service engine. These remedies will include not just technical approaches associated with the core product or service including perhaps elements of the ITIL v3 operations framework, a new development methodology or platform technologies but a richer combination of remedies demanding the greater range of skills as demanded by the service engine. Repeated use of the approach will eventually close the gaps between the business need and IT without necessarily expecting the business to formally define its objectives as we asked them to do in the early IT strategy methodologies.

Where we have been retained to introduce business change (i.e. where the primary focus is not IT) we have been able to realign IT by using these 'business-focused IT' frameworks. This has ranged from developing new strategies for IT including new applications and changes to the technical architecture based on the changes to the business requirement to the complete outsourcing IT with a clear brief to the supplier on what is required by the business. The advantage of this to a change manager is that they retain control of a key element of the change programme.

Regardless of the start point, we can expect a 'business-focused IT' approach to yield a huge productivity gain in terms of introducing performance improvement. We can also expect a much greater range of possible remedies than we might be used to and these can be used in combination for greater impact. The cost of some can be modest yet the impact can be significant, especially when dealing with improved business awareness, improved marketing and communication, greater value, improved organisation, better accountability, reduced costs etc. Just consider two extremes: adding good communications to a major change programme can add little cost but make the difference between success and failure whilst managing in a wholly technical way will almost always result in failure.

A true business-focused approach to IT will always appear to be more relevant to the business because it always demonstrably addresses business needs and gaps. If this relevance can be combined with a greater awareness (of the market) and greater agility (rapid implementation) then the service would be perceived to be as good as if the business was able to react instantly to new requirements by doing these things for itself.

5 A New Maturity Model

A number of organisations have developed maturity models. Maturity models have been around since the 1970s and started by describing the early stages of the development of the data processing organisation and later the IT era. They all reflect a view of the evolution of a particular technology or the extent to which we have defined and automated process (which is probably dependent upon a particular technology). Traditional maturity models mostly describe a process by which we will achieve maturity without being specific about how the outcome might look or feel. The capability maturity model for example describes how we must progress through ad-hoc management, repeatable processes, defined and standardised processes to having managed and optimised processes. With few exceptions they describe the final stage as being business-driven or with the end user as the driving force; unfortunately they do not describe what this is, what it means, what we have to do to achieve it or how we might know when we have achieved it.

Today we develop strategy, specify the requirement in detail, take some weeks to select a supplier and then impose stringent and bureaucratic controls on our suppliers during the delivery phases. We approach large projects and programmes with fixed specifications and rigid methodology such that the service provider is unable to respond to the many changes in requirement, changes in technology and changes in personnel that will take place during the life of the programme. Defining final stages of maturity as some kind of advanced state of ossification of some inappropriate IT process that rarely, if ever, worked is not sensible.

Perhaps it is time to redefine the maturity model. At the outset we identified a linear or power law relationship between 'closeness to the business' and success. From the preceding pages we can perhaps assume that a linear relationship may be an approximation to the total business experience (i.e. success is more likely where the total business experience is high). If the relationship is more of an exponential one perhaps it can be expressed by total business experience squared. When we introduced the service excellence model we were essentially looking at the service requirement gap, the gap between the business need and the service specification. This was then broken down into the detail of how the service is delivered (which encompasses all of the core services and brand equity considerations) as well as the detail of how the business plans for the investment and the deployment as part of a business planning process. This model is unlikely to change though the business environment and the underlying technologies will. To be sure that we are delivering what is needed by the business, the needs, the total business experience and the service spec would need to be the same. Putting this another way we need to be able to set a service specification that accurately reflects what the business wants and then we must deliver this using a service engine that is ultra-efficient so that there is little or no difference between the service specification and the total business experience. Using the assessment framework we can say quite explicitly that an ultra-efficient service engine will look like that illustrated in Figure 5.1. Given the above we can then simplify the service excellence model to the bare basics and consider this to be the new maturity model (see Figure 5.2).

The final stage of maturity is not to be business-driven if we mean by this that that service providers must do as the business says. It has never really worked that way. Mostly the start is some kind of expression of a business requirement. This is followed by developing what can be achieved technically and what may be available. This may be followed by a modified (perhaps more informed) requirement thus creating new needs and increasing the service requirement gap. At the same time the business and the service provider will be hard at work using the service excellence model to narrow the gaps between needs, business planning, and service specification. The ultra-efficient service engine will deliver a revised business experience. The skills of our service providers and the resources at their disposal will not be limited to just the development of the delivery of the service but extend into all areas yielding a high total business experience and business and IT will be intimately realigned though business planning and investment will always be under business control. Services organisations will be more relevant, agile and aware. We will all be more adept at recognising when we need to introduce big change or incremental improvement and know how to plan and deliver this rapidly and successfully. We will be adept at developing strategic relationships with supply organisations and recognising when these need to end. We will be capable of exploiting innovation. Communications skills will be fine tuned to both receive and transmit. The needs of particularly difficult sectors and situations will be better understood. Businesses and services organisations will have a better understanding of what has to be done to achieve alignment without unnecessary intellectualisation. Outside the business we can hope that standards and methods have caught up and are of a higher quality. All of this requires an intimacy between the service providers and the business and so productivity, not cheapness, will become king; in the final stages of maturity we will be achieving immediate business change closing the service requirement gap as quickly as it is identified. One way in which this can be achieved is through greater automation and by unifying the business and the service provider but how it is to be achieved is immaterial provided all gaps are closed leaving no requirement outstanding.

FIGURE 5.1 *The ultra-efficient service engine*

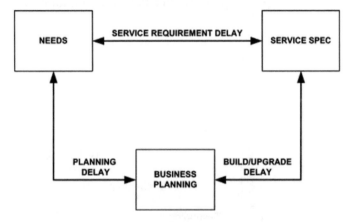

FIGURE 5.2 *The new maturity model*

In fact in this new maturity model, gaps will become more time related (i.e. they can be expected to closed quickly) and so we refer not to 'gaps' but to 'delays'. Where a service requirement gap itself arises it is likely to be small and not always negative. This will arise for two principal reasons. First when we need additional capacity it tends to come in increments that will exceed what additional capacity is required. Second because new technologies will emerge which provide more capability than we can immediately exploit. There will usually be an awareness of something new before it is made available to the business and the new technology will always promise improved performance or stimulate new demand of some kind. Thus there may be an over-provision of service until demand catches up.

Foster (1986) described the technology 'S-curve' which supports the second of these. Foster's theory describes technological progression as a series of lifecycle curves resembling an 'S' shape. S-curves are derived by plotting the performance of the technology against the effort invested; over time curves can overlap each other. We have known about S-curves for some time; Gibson and Nolan (1974) used S-curves to describe the phases of organisational learning and expenditure in relation to data processing. Rogers (1962) theorised that innovations would spread through society in an S-curve, slowly at first, then gathering momentum, until in the later stages as the market saturates or the product has less attraction we see little growth. Today, consciously or subconsciously, we manage complex, relatively short, concurrent and overlapping technology S-curves. Sometimes there can be a discontinuity between technologies when reinvestment is required but otherwise we see a steady incremental investment. As each new technology emerges performance is slow, at its peak it is experiencing exponential improvement and into maturity the performance tails off. Technology S-curves are illustrated in Figure 5.3.

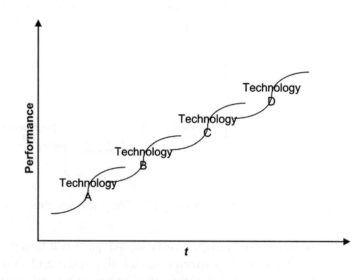

FIGURE 5.3 *Technology S-curves*

In a perfect market of the supply and demand of service to a business delivered by an ultra-efficient service engine, this under- and over-provision of either capacity or changes in technology should be small unless there is serious discontinuity between the technologies. This is illustrated in Figure 5.4.

We always express views of the future from today's mindset and yet when we arrive it is always different. Very generalised models such as the capability maturity model will continue to apply and we know that we are

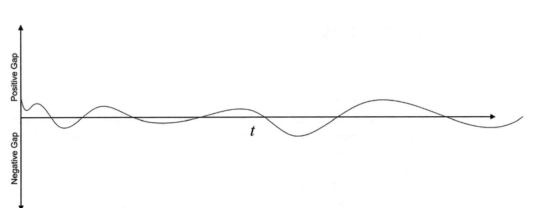

FIGURE 5.4   *Under- and over-provision of service in a complex adaptive system*

seeking a state of continuous process improvement but we struggle to understand what processes we will be deploying. Thus we are considering how the maturity model will look at some point in the future when we know that both the requirement and the technical solution will change. The biggest change will be the way we measure the success of what is achieved. By shortening the service requirement delay we know that we will also achieve both alignment and value-add to the business.

6 Summary

Many notable organisations including major consultancies, hardware vendors and government agencies have developed models and standards to describe aspects of IT management best practice. They include strategy development, programme or project management, IT service management and IT governance.

The array of methods is astonishing but as good as they are they are incomplete. Without exception they focus on how to do 'IT things' and have so far ignored the importance of business outcome and business opinion. One or two of the maturity models mention that the aim is ultimately to become business-driven but there is no explanation to drive implementation. These methodologies are mostly the manifestation of the application of the 'people, process and technology mantra' to IT itself. They are 'left-brained' solutions (for 'left-brained' people) and we should recognise their limitations.

It may have taken those of us in IT a little longer to appreciate that buyers do not buy drills but holes. The concept of 'business-focused IT' is not a revolutionary development but it does move the focus inextricably from IT methods to business value. No matter what we do or how we do it, the acid test is whether it meets the business need. By refocusing on the business we can radically improve delivery.

We must continue to drive for excellence by applying (IT) best practice but be intolerant of poor processes, methods and standards that fail to improve performance and outcomes. We should reconnect with the business through applying relevance, agility and awareness and then measure our performance as the business does (i.e. on outcomes). We should identify and close all gaps by referencing the service excellence model, use the assessment framework for the service engine on a regular basis, manage our brand, manage the core product, be comfortable with subjective measures as well as quantifiable performance metrics and manage an active improvement and outcome programme. We must prepare for the future by being better at business and better at communicating. We must constantly review and improve the business (and IT) model by using techniques such as the strategy framework.

From now on, IT service providers must strive to achieve service excellence because this is the means to achieving greater business success. Longer term, IT people will become the business and so will create the ultra-efficient service engine. Automation as always will play its part in this but business-focused IT tells us that not only must it respond quickly to the mechanics of business change but it must also be capable of dealing with the commercial, emotional and functional needs of the right brain.

References

Ambler, T. (2006) Stepping stones. *The Marketer (Magazine of the Chartered Institute of Marketing)*, 28, 18 October.

Beinhocker, E. (2007) *The origin of wealth.* Random House Business Books, London. ISBN: 978-0712676618.

Burke, R. (1999) *Project management and control techniques* (3rd edition). John Wiley & Sons, New York. ISBN: 047198762X.

Buzan, T. (2001) *Head strong.* HarperCollins, London. ISBN: 978-0007113962.

Carlzon, J. (1989) *Moments of truth.* HarperCollins, London. ISBN: 0060915803.

Christopher, M., Payne, A. and Ballantyne, D. (1991) *Relationship marketing.* Butterworth-Heinemann, Oxford. ISBN: 0750609788.

Cialdini, R. B. (2000) *Influence: science and practice* (4th edition). Allyn and Bacon, London. ISBN: 0321011473.

Claus, W. J. (1991) *Veranden van organisatieculturen: het krachtenmodel.* Scriptum Management, Scheidam.

Coker, D. M., Del Gaizo, E. R., Murray, K. A. and Edwards, S. L. (2002) *High performance sales organizations: creating competitive advantage in the global marketplace.* McGraw-Hill, New York. ISBN: 0071367624.

Daffy, C. (1999) *Once a customer, always a customer* (2nd edition). Oak Tree Press, Cork. ISBN: 978-1860761645.

Dalrymple, D. J., Cron, W. L. and DeCarlo, T. E. (2001) *Sales management: concepts and cases* (7th edition). John Wiley & Sons, New York. ISBN: 0471388807.

Davidson, H. (2002) *The committed enterprise.* Butterworth-Heinemann, Oxford. ISBN: 978-0750655408.

Feldman, P. and Miller, D. (1986) Entity model clustering: structuring a data model by abstraction. *Comput. J.,* 29, 348–360.

Foster, R. (1986) *Innovation: the attacker's advantage.* Summit Books, New York. ISBN: 0333435117.

Gad, T. (2001) *4-D branding: cracking the code of network branding.* Prentice-Hall, Englewood Cliffs, NJ. ISBN: 0273653687.

Gibson, C. F. and Nolan, R. L. (1974) Managing the four stages of EDP growth. *Harvard Business Rev.*, 52(1), 76–88.

Godin, S. (2002) *Unleashing the ideavirus.* Simon and Schuster, London. ISBN: 978-0743220651.

Goldratt, E. (1997) *Critical chain: a business novel.* Gower, Aldershot. ISBN: 0884271536.

Hammer, M. (1996) *Beyond re-engineering: how the process-centred organisation is changing our work and our lives.* Profile Books, London. ISBN: 978-1861975188.

Handy, C. (1996) *Gods of management.* Oxford University Press, New York. ISBN: 0195096177.

Harrison, L. E. and Huntingdon, S. P. (2000). GNP per capita from World Bank estimates of purchasing power parity, in 1995 U.S. dollars. Reproduced in Beinhocker (2000).

Harvey Nash (2007) Capabilities of the IT team. *The Harvey Nash USA and KPMG 2006/2007 Strategic Leadership Survey - a CIO perspective.* http://www.harveynash.com/usa/services/it_services/cio.asp

Hoar, R. (2005). Be more persuasive. *Management Today*, March, pp. 56–59.

Holt, J. and Newton, J. (2004) *A managers guide to IT law.* British Computer Society, Swindon. ISBN: 1902505557.

Horovitz, J. (2000) *Seven secrets of service strategy.* Prentice-Hall, Englewood Cliffs, NJ. ISBN: 0273635778.

Hughes, B., Ireland, R., West, B., Smith, N. and Shepherd, D. I. (2004) *Project management for IT-related projects: textbook for the ISEB Foundation Certificate in IS Project Management.* British Computer Society, Swindon. ISBN: 978-1902505589.

ITIL (2007) *The official introduction to the ITIL lifecycle.* The Stationery Office, London. ISBN: 978-0113310616.

Juran, J. M. and Gryna, F. M. (1993) *Quality planning and analysis.* McGraw-Hill, New York, pp. 5–6.

Kalakota, R. and Robinson, M. (1999) *e-Business - roadmap for success.* Addison-Wesley, Reading, MA. ISBN: 0201604809.

Kaplan, R. S. and Norton, D. P. (1996) *The balanced scorecard: translating strategy into action.* Harvard Business School Press, Boston, MA. ISBN: 0875846513.

Kaplan, R. S. and Norton, D. P. (2004) *Strategy maps: converting intangible assets into tangible outcomes.* Harvard Business School Press, Boston, MA. ISBN: 1591391342.

Kaplan, R. S. and Norton, D. P. (2006) *Alignment: using the balanced scorecard to create corporate synergies.* Harvard Business School Press, Boston, MA. ISBN: 1591396905.

Kets de Vries, M. F. R. and Miller, D. (1991). *The neurotic organization: diagnosing and revitalizing unhealthy companies.* HarperCollins, London. ISBN: 0887304885.

Kirby, J. and Marsden, P. (2006) *Connected marketing.* Elsevier, Amsterdam. ISBN: 075066634X.

Kolah, A. (2002) *Essential law for marketers.* Butterworth-Heinemann, Oxford. ISBN: 0750655003.

Kotler, P., Hayes, T. and Bloom, P. N. (2002) *Marketing professional services* (2nd edition). Prentice-Hall, Englewood Cliffs, NJ. ISBN: 073520179X.

Levitt, T. (1960) Marketing myopia. *Harvard Business Rev.,* July/August, pp. 3–23.

Liker, J. K. (2005) *The Toyota way.* McGraw-Hill, New York. ISBN: 0071392319.

Miller, R. B., Heiman, S. E. and Tuleja, T. (1994) *Successful large account management.* Kogan Page, Philadelphia, PA. ISBN: 0749414049.

Milner, D. (1995) *Success in advertising and promotion.* John Murray, London. ISBN: 0719553717.

Moore, G. A. (1991) *Crossing the chasm.* HarperBusiness, London. ISBN: 0060517123.

Morton, C. (1994) *Becoming world class.* Macmillan, London. ISBN: 0333625609.

Mudie, P. and Cottam, A. (1993) The management and marketing of services. Butterworth-Heinemann, Oxford. ISBN: 0750635940.

Parasuraman, A., Zeithaml, V. A. and Berry, L. L. (1985) A conceptual model of service quality and its implications for future research. *J. Marketing,* 49(4), 41–50.

Peters, T. (2003) *Re-imagine! Business excellence in a disruptive age.* Dorling Kindersley, London. ISBN: 1405300493.

Porter, M. E. (1985). *Advantage: creating and sustaining superior performance.* The Free Press, New York. ISBN: 0029250900.

Quinn, R. E. and Rohrbaugh, J. (1983). A spatial model of effectiveness criteria: towards a competing values approach to organizational analysis. *Management Sci.,* 29, 363–377.

Rackham, N. (1995) *SPIN selling.* Gower, Aldershot. ISBN: 0566076896.

Ridderstråle, J. and Nordström, K. (2002) *Funky business* (2nd edition). Financial Times Management, London. ISBN: 978-0273659075.

Ries, A. and Trout, J. (1993) *The 22 immutable laws of marketing.* HarperCollins, London. ISBN: 978-0006383451.

Ries, A. and Trout, J. (2001) *Positioning: the battle for your mind.* McGraw-Hill, New York. ISBN: 0071373586.

Rogers, E. M. (1962) *Diffusion of innovations (4th edition).* The Free Press, New York. ISBN: 0028740742.

Sherrington, M. (2003) *Added value - the alchemy of brand-led growth.* Palgrave Macmillan, London. ISBN: 1403903875.

Smith, B. (2005) *Making marketing happen.* Elsevier, Amsterdam. ISBN: 0750662484.

Tapscot, D. and Williams, A. D. (2007) *Wikinomics - how mass collaboration changes everything.* Atlantic Books, London. ISBN: 978-1843546368.

ten Have, S. (2002). *Voorbeeldig veranden: een kwestie van organiseren, proefschrift.* Twente University, Amsterdam: Uitgeverij Nieuweijds.

ten Have, S., ten Have, W., Stevens, F. and van der Elst, M. (2003). *Key management models.* Financial Times Press, London. ISBN: 0273662015.

Treacy, M. and Wiersema, F. (1995). *The discipline of market leaders.* Addison-Wesley, Reading, MA. ISBN: 0201406489.

Weber, C. V. Paulk, M. C. Wise, C. J. and Withey, J. W. (1991) Key practices of the capability maturity model. *Technical report CMU/SEi-91-TR-025,* Pittsburgh Software Engineering Institute.

Index

BUSINESS-FOCUSED IT & SERVICE EXCELLENCE 2nd Edition
DAVID MILLER

NEW

A revolutionary, new service excellence model that creates more accurate alignment between service providers and business customers, is central to this radical re-think on service delivery. IT remains crucial to the on-going success of most businesses, and David Miller's new model helps service providers gain a clear understanding of the businesses they seek to serve.

www.bcs.org/books/businessfocus Published: May 2008

Price: **£24.95** 238pp

ISBN: 978-1-902505-88-6

WORLD CLASS IT SERVICE DELIVERY
PETER WHEATCROFT

The practical manual that helps you achieve and maintain new standards in service delivery. Written from a real-life business perspective, it supports the *ISEB Service Management Certificate* and is essential for IT managers, executives and consultants in the process of raising their service standards, considering offshoring or moving towards the ultimate goal of 24x7 service excellence. "A mindset for how IT should engage with business" *(Information Age)*.

www.bcs.org/books/servicedelivery Published: Apr 2007

Price: **£24.95** 192pp

ISBN: 978-1-902505-82-4

INVISIBLE ARCHITECTURE
JENNY URE and GUDRUN JAEGERSBERG

Designing and building new IT systems, means you are likely to face specific challenges. Quite often the biggest of these are not the technical but the 'socio-technical', especially when implementing across national borders. Through the use of real life examples, *Invisible Architecture* shows how you can actually harness these 'soft' factors to give you that competitive advantage. The potential consequences of ignoring these problems are also exposed.

www.bcs.org/books/invisiblearchitecture Published: Mar 2005

Price: **£34.95** 100pp

ISBN: 978-1-902505-59-6

IT-ENABLED BUSINESS CHANGE An ISEB Foundation

SHARM MANWANI

NEW

The high profile failure of major IT-related projects in both public and private sectors underlines the need for stringent change management. As businesses increasingly look to IT to enable that change, this book examines the types of business change processes that involve the use of IT, from the reasons organisations change the way they work, to how that change is managed and implemented.

IT Enabled
Business Change
An ISEB Foundation

Sharm Manwani

www.bcs.org/books/businesschange Published: May 2008

Price: **£24.95** 236pp

ISBN: 978-1-902505-91-6

BUSINESS PROCESS MANAGEMENT

MARTYN A OULD

BCS

Business Process Management

A Rigorous Approach

Martyn A Ould

Businesses adapt constantly to ensure they stay ahead of the game, but often they are held back by static IT systems dictating process and procedure. By learning how your organisation operates, and what activities and processes are carried out within it, you begin to understand the business more fully and can build better, more flexible IT systems to support improved efficiency and drive profitability.

www.bcs.org/books/bpm Published: Jan 2005

Price: **£34.95** 360pp

ISBN: 978-1-902505-60-2

A PRAGMATIC GUIDE TO BUSINESS PROCESS MODELLING

JON HOLT

Improving processes, productivity and profitability within your organisation is often best achieved by having a detailed knowledge of business process modelling. It is considered a core competency for anyone involved in managing change and Jon Holt's expert text explores all the main aspects including process analysis and process documentation. Applying the standard modelling notation (UML), the result is a detailed, step-by-step guide to the entire modelling process.

BCS

A Pragmatic Guide to
Business Process Modelling

Jon Holt

www.bcs.org/books/processmodelling Published: Sep 2005

Price: **£29.95** 188pp

ISBN: 978-1-902505-66-4

INFORMATION SECURITY MANAGEMENT PRINCIPLES

NEW

ANDY TAYLOR (Editor)

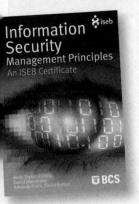

How safe is your information? Recent events show that commercial, personal and sensitive information is very hard to keep secure and technological solutions are not the only answer. Information security is largely a management issue and this book outlines the management principles for securing your data. It also acts as a textbook for the *ISEB Information Security Management Principles Certificate.*

www.bcs.org/books/informationsecurity Published: Jun 2008

Price: **£24.95** 256pp

ISBN: 978-1-902505-90-9

PRINCIPLES OF DATA MANAGEMENT

KEITH GORDON

Organisations increasingly view data as a valuable corporate asset and its effective management can be vital to your organisation's success. This professional reference guide covers all the key areas including database development, data quality and corporate data modelling. It is not based on a particular proprietary system, so is business focused, providing the knowledge and techniques required for you to successfully implement the data management function.

www.bcs.org/books/datamanagement Published: Aug 2007

Price: **£29.95** 272pp

ISBN: 978-1-902505-84-8

PRACTICAL DATA MIGRATION

JOHN MORRIS

Ensuring the success of your data migration projects is crucial, especially if you are looking to achieve maximum return on your investment. By following the best practice model devised by author John Morris, this guide will help you ensure a smooth and problem-free migration. The guide contains techniques and strategies, blended with real-life examples and clear definitions of the most commonly used terminology.

www.bcs.org/books/datamigration Published: Apr 2006

Price: **£29.95** 224pp

ISBN: 978-1-902505-71-8

DATA PROTECTION & COMPLIANCE IN CONTEXT

STEWART ROOM

Large-scale data loss continues to make headline news, highlighting the need for stringent data protection policies, especially when personal or commercially sensitive information is at stake. This title provides detailed analysis of current data protection laws and discusses compliance issues, before providing you with a platform on which to build internal compliance strategies. The author is chair of the National Association of Data Protection Officers (NADPO).

www.bcs.org/books/dataprotection Published: Nov 2006

Price: **£34.95** 304pp
ISBN: 978-1-902505-78-7

IT LAW An ISEB Foundation

JON FELL (Editor)

Breaking the law can be costly, so it is vital IT professionals understand their legal obligations amid the deluge of legislation governing information technology. This publication covers the main aspects of law specifically applicable to IT, including digital evidence, data protection, and corporate governance. Designed to help prevent serious legal breaches, it is also the only official textbook of the *ISEB Foundation Certificate in IT Law*.

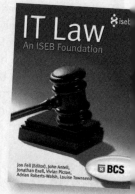

www.bcs.org/books/isebitlaw Published: Nov 2007

Price: **£24.95** 320pp
ISBN: 978-1-902505-80-0

A MANAGER'S GUIDE TO IT LAW

JEREMY NEWTON and JEREMY HOLT (Editors)

Businesses face a legal minefield when it comes to information technology, with legislation covering issues as diverse as data protection, IT procurement, outsourcing and joint ventures. This guide provides plain-English explanations of all the relevant legislation, and includes examples from actual case law. "It is readable and provides practical advice . . . a valuable addition to my bookshelf" (*British Journal of Healthcare Computing & Information Management*).

www.bcs.org/books/itlaw Published: Jul 2004

Price: **£29.95** 176pp
ISBN: 978-1-902505-55-8

ORDER FORM

⊞ BCS

Business-Focused IT and Service Excellence – 2nd Ed (May-08) _____

World Class IT Service Delivery _____

Invisible Architecture _____

IT-Enabled Business Change (May-08) _____

Business Process Management _____

A Pragmatic Guide to Business Process Modelling _____

Information Security Management Principles: An ISEB Certificate (Jun-08) _____

Principles of Data Management _____

Practical Data Migration _____

Data Protection & Compliance in Context _____

IT Law: An ISEB Foundation _____

A Manager's Guide to IT Law _____

Electronic Business – 2nd Ed (May-08) _____

The World Beyond Digital Rights Management _____

Software Testing: An ISEB Foundation _____

Project Management in the Real World _____

Project Management for IT-Related Projects: An ISEB Foundation _____

Professional Issues in Information Technology _____

IT Procurement Handbook for SMEs _____

Finance for IT Decision Makers – 2nd Ed _____

Business Analysis _____

Global Services _____

A Guide To Global Sourcing _____

BCS Glossary of Computing and ICT – 12th Ed (Sep-08) _____

P&P: UK £2.75 for the first book, then 75p for each additional item. Europe €7.50 then €1.00 for each additional item. Rest of the world $24.00 then $2.00 for each additional item.

BCS Books are available in all good bookshops.
To order direct, please complete this form and send it to:
BCS Books, Turpin Distribution, Pegasus Drive,
Stratton Business Park, Biggleswade,
Bedfordshire, SG18 8TQ, UK.
Fax: +44 (0)1767 601640 Tel: +44 (0)1767 604951
Enquiries to: custserv@turpin-distribution.com

GBP	BCS Member	Qty	
£24.95	£20.00		Title .... Initials ....
£24.95	£20.00		Surname ....
£34.95	£25.00		Delivery address ....
£24.95	£20.00		....
£34.95	£30.00		Telephone ....
£29.95	£25.00		Email ....
£24.95	£20.00		BCS membership number (if applicable) ....
£29.95	£25.00		I enclose a cheque ☐ made payable to
£29.95	£25.00		**'The British Computer Society'** or please charge my:
£34.95	£30.00		☐ Visa ☐ Mastercard ☐ Switch/Maestro
£24.95	£20.00		☐ **American Express** (please indicate)
£29.95	£25.00		Start date (Maestro/Switch only) ....
£24.95	£20.00		Issue number (Maestro/Switch only) ....
£24.95	£20.00		Expiry date ....
£24.95	£20.00		Card number ....
£24.95	£20.00		Name as it appears on card ....
£24.95	£20.00		Card holders' address (if different from delivery address)
£24.95	£20.00		....
£29.95	£25.00		....
£34.95	£25.00		Signature ....
£29.95	£25.00		
£29.95	£20.00		*BooksUpdate service: please mark this box to receive*
£34.95	£25.00		*occasional emails about new titles and special offers on*
£19.95	£15.00		*BCS publications (you can opt out from receiving these*
Sub - Total			*communications at any time).* ☐
P&P			**Please note:** Information is correct at the time of going to press. However it is subject to change without notice. MEM0108
Total			

ELECTRONIC BUSINESS 2nd Edition

GEOFFREY SAMPSON

As technology continues to drive changes in the way we do business,
more companies rely on electronic tools to carry out an increasing
array of business functions. IT professionals have a greater role to play
in the success of electronic businesses, and Geoffrey Sampson provides an
overview of the main aspects, enabling you to have a better
understanding of how IT and business interact.

www.bcs.org/books/electronicbusiness Published: May 2008

Price: **£24.95** 238pp

ISBN: 978-1-902505-89-3

THE WORLD BEYOND DIGITAL RIGHTS MANAGEMENT

JUDE UMEH

The battle to protect intellectual property and commercial rights
remains fierce, with digital content owners and commercial stakeholders
under constant threat from piracy, file-sharing networks and illegal
downloads. Content creators, law makers and businesses must learn to
work with the end-user, if the fantastic opportunities presented in this
book are to be harnessed. Jude Umeh reveals how current practices
must give way to a post-DRM future.

www.bcs.org/books/drm Published: Oct 2007

Price: **£24.95** 320pp

ISBN: 978-1-902505-87-9

SOFTWARE TESTING An ISEB Foundation

BRIAN HAMBLING (Editor)

The bestselling software testing title and the only official textbook of
the *ISEB Foundation Certificate in Software Testing*. This title covers
the main functions of the testing process and provides you with the
practical insight needed to perform effective tests. Includes worked
examples and sample questions. "Invaluable for anyone involved in
testing and would lift the game of most VV&T staff"
(*IT Training Magazine*).

www.bcs.org/books/softwaretesting Revised: Mar 2008

Price: **£24.95** 224pp

ISBN: 978-1-902505-79-4

PROJECT MANAGEMENT IN THE REAL WORLD

ELIZABETH HARRIN

Fast forward to professional project management, with this ultimate short-cut. It summarises over 250 years of expertise from experienced project managers and offers hints and tips on all aspects of project management including how to manage budgets, manage teams and manage yourself. These are backed up with theory and references alongside case studies from the UK, USA, France, Holland and Australia. "Good common sense stuff" (*Health Informatics Now*).

www.bcs.org/books/realworldPM Published: Nov 2006

Price: **£24.95** 232pp

ISBN: 978-1-902505-81-7

PROJECT MANAGEMENT FOR IT-RELATED PROJECTS

BOB HUGHES (Editor)

Covers subjects ranging from project planning, monitoring and control to change management, risk management and communication between project stakeholders. Each chapter includes an overview of learning objectives, details of syllabus content, activities and multiple choice questions, so you can carry out self-assessment exercises and measure your own performance. Covers the entire syllabus of the *ISEB Foundation Certificate in IS Project Management*.

www.bcs.org/books/projectmanagement Published: Aug 2004

Price: **£24.95** 148pp

ISBN: 978-1-902505-58-9

PROFESSIONAL ISSUES IN INFORMATION TECHNOLOGY

FRANK BOTT

This book explores the relationship between technological change, society and the law, and the powerful role that computers and computer professionals play in a technological society. Designed to accompany the BCS Professional Examination Core Diploma Module: *Professional Issues in Information Systems Practice*. The author is former Head of Computer Science at the University of Wales, and has previously lectured at the University of Missouri.

www.bcs.org/books/professionalissues Published: May 2005

Price: **£24.95** 264pp

ISBN: 978-1-902505-65-7

IT PROCUREMENT HANDBOOK FOR SMEs

NEW

DAVID NICKSON

Large organisations can suffer badly when IT procurement goes wrong, but for Small-Medium Enterprises (SMEs), it can be fatal. David Nickson guides you through the entire procurement process. Whether you are identifying the changing IT requirements of your business, evaluating potential suppliers or managing them once appointed, this handbook means you can avoid the pitfalls which have led to the ruin of so many SMEs.

www.bcs.org/books/procurement Published: Feb 2008

Price: **£29.95** 208pp
ISBN: 978-1-902505-98-5

FINANCE FOR IT DECISION MAKERS 2nd Edition

MICHAEL BLACKSTAFF

A no-nonsense, step-by-step guide to the areas of finance as they relate to IT. Assuming no prior knowledge of finance, this guide teaches you how to construct a financial case for IT projects and covers other areas such as methods of financing, current legislation, cost/benefit analysis, budgeting, costing and pricing. It is designed for both business and non-commercial organisations, and is ideal for managers, practitioners, buyers, sellers and consultants.

www.bcs.org/books/finance Published: Jul 2006

Price: **£34.95** 344pp
ISBN: 978-1-902505-73-2

BUSINESS ANALYSIS

DEBRA PAUL and DONALD YEATES (Editors)

Improving the effectiveness of your IT through better alignment with the business is a precursor to increasing profitability. This practical, introductory guide provides you with the tools to achieve this. It teaches you about strategy analysis and how to model business systems and processes and covers other topics including business case development, change management, and engineering/information resource management. The book also supports the *ISEB Diploma in Business Analysis*.

www.bcs.org/books/businessanalysis Published: Apr 2006

Price: **£29.95** 256pp
ISBN: 978-1-902505-70-1

GLOBAL SERVICES

MARK KOBAYASHI-HILLARY and DR RICHARD SYKES

Global
Services
Moving to a Level
Playing Field

Mark Kobayashi - Hillary
and Richard Sykes

BCS

Globalisation of the service industry can help transform your business and open up new opportunities for your industry. Outsourcing gurus Kobayshi-Hillary and Sykes deliver a groundbreaking assessment of the factors that can help shape this, through the creation of a new framework. "A valuable, thought-provoking resource for any organisation working with an IT services budget - whether a provider or a consumer of those services" (*Information Age*)

www.bcs.org/books/globalservices Published: Apr 2007

Price: **£29.95** 224pp
ISBN: 978-1-902505-83-1

A GUIDE TO GLOBAL SOURCING

ELIZABETH ANNE SPARROW

Commercial organisations are increasingly looking at outsourcing and offshoring to help manage costs and improve efficiencies. Elizabeth Sparrow offers a detailed examination of the opportunities and obstacles you are likely to face when considering outsourcing, and includes a country-by-country assessment of offshore services. Other global delivery models are also considered, including setting up joint ventures or shared service centres and acquiring overseas companies.

BCS®
THE BRITISH COMPUTER SOCIETY

A Guide to
Global
Sourcing

Offshore outsourcing and
other global delivery models

Elizabeth Anne
Sparrow

www.bcs.org/books/globalsourcing Published: Nov 2004

Price: **£34.95** 192pp
ISBN: 978-1-902505-61-9

ABOUT THE PUBLISHER

The British Computer Society is the leading professional body for the IT industry, with more than 60,000 members in over 100 countries. It is the qualifying body for Chartered IT Professionals (CITP) and promotes the study and practice of computing for the benefit of society as a whole. BCS Books publishes a range of titles designed to support business managers, IT professionals and students.

CALL FOR AUTHORS

The BCS welcomes proposals from potential authors for books at the business/ IT interface. If you are interested in writing a book for the BCS please visit: www.bcs.org/books/writer for more information or contact Matthew Flynn by emailing him at: matthew.flynn@hq.bcs.org.uk

BCS Glossary
of Computing and ICT

- Bestselling and internationally renowned, now in its 12th Edition
- Over 3,000 terms clearly defined and explained in context
- Supports the National Curriculum and National Qualifications Framework
- Fully indexed and cross-referenced throughout, for easy access
- Compiled by experts at the British Computer Society

The BCS Glossary is the most authoritative and comprehensive glossary of its kind on the market today. This unrivalled study aid and reference tool has newly updated entries and is divided into themed sections making it more than just a list of definitions. Written in a style that is easily accessible to anybody with an interest in computing, it is specifically designed to support those taking computer courses or courses where computers are used, including GCSE, A-Level, ECDL and 14-19 Diplomas in Functional Skills in schools and Further Education Colleges.

The Glossary has been compiled by members of the British Computer Society Education and Training Expert Panel, many of whom are teachers or former teachers. In creating the Glossary, they have drawn heavily upon their many years of experience in the education sector as well as their detailed knowledge of computing. The resulting definitions, and the way they are organised, help the reader build up a knowledge and understanding of computing.

TWELFTH EDITION

BCS Glossary
of Computing and ICT

BCS

£19.95 450pp

Published: SEP 2008
ISBN: 978-1-906124-00-7

www.bcs.org/books/bcsglossary